SUPERVILLAINS v SUPERHEROES A-Z

SUPERVILLAINS v SUPERHEROES A-Z

SARAH OLIVER

JOHN BLAKE

Published by John Blake Publishing Ltd,
3 Bramber Court, 2 Bramber Road,
London W14 9PB, England

www.johnblakepublishing.co.uk

www.facebook.com/Johnblakepub facebook
twitter.com/johnblakepub twitter

First published in paperback in 2011

ISBN: 978 1 84358 420 9

British Library Cataloguing-in-Publication Data:

A catalogue record for this book is available from the British Library.

Design by www.envydesign.co.uk

Printed and bound by CPI Group (UK) Ltd, Croydon, CR0 4YY

3 5 7 9 10 8 6 4 2

Papers used by John Blake Publishing are natural, recyclable products made from
wood grown in sustainable forests. The manufacturing processes conform to the
environmental regulations of the country of origin.

Every attempt has been made to contact the relevant copyright-holders,
but some were unobtainable. We would be grateful if the appropriate
people could contact us.

ABOUT THE AUTHOR

Sarah Oliver is a journalist who loves Superhero movies. Her favourite three Supervillains of all time are Mystique, the Green Goblin and Abomination. This book is dedicated to her husband Jon who helped with the writing and editing of this book. His favourite three Supervillains are Lex Luthor, Venom and Sabretooth.

OTHER A-Z BOOKS BY SARAH OLIVER

Justin Bieber A–Z
The Wanted A–Z
One Direction A–Z
Taylor Lautner A–Z
Robert Pattinson A–Z
The Completely Unofficial *Glee* A–Z
Miley Cyrus A-Z

SUPERVILLAINS A-Z

THE ULTIMATE GUIDE TO THE GREATEST SUPERVILLAINS OF ALL TIME

This book is jam-packed with the biggest and best Supervillains there have ever been. We've carefully selected over 60 of your favourite Supervillains to be in this *Supervillains A–Z*!

It includes all your DC favourites like the Joker and Lex Luthor, and all your favourite Marvel villains like Magneto and Red Skull. There are plenty of new Supervillains that you might never have heard of before but who will be appearing in the new Superhero movies that are coming to cinemas soon!

If you want to learn about the new X-Men mutants or find out more about who Spider-Man will be facing in the next movie, then you'll find it all inside. You'll discover all the behind-the-scenes secrets, the problems certain actors had to overcome, and how they went about filming the fight sequences. You can also find out the history behind the characters and which Supervillains have been around for the longest.

You can read this book from start to finish, or dip in and out of it, as you prefer. Once you've read all about the greatest Supervillains of all time, flip the book over and learn all about their enemies in *Superheroes A–Z*.

A IS FOR...

ABOMINATION (EMIL BLONSKY)

 Appears in: *The Incredible Hulk* (2008)

Powers: Super-strength, bulletproof skin

First comic-book appearance: April 1967

Abomination is the monster that is created when Royal Marines Commando Emil Blonsky takes super-soldier serum and some of Bruce Banner's blood in a bid to be as powerful as the Hulk.

Emil is the main villain in *The Incredible Hulk* and proves to be a tough opponent. He is only defeated when the Hulk manages to wrap chains around him and almost chokes him to death.

The actor chosen to play Abomination and Emil Blonsky in *The Incredible Hulk* was Tim Roth. He was accustomed to playing evil characters having played the barbaric Thade in *Planet of the*

Apes (2001) and murderer Archibald Cunningham in *Rob Roy* (1995).

DID YOU KNOW?

Tim Roth was originally picked to play Professor Snape in the Harry Potter movies but he had to back out because he was filming *Planet of the Apes* at the time and didn't feel comfortable switching from one to the other. He wanted to concentrate all his efforts on playing Thade.

Tim loved playing Emil even though it wasn't the easiest part in the world – it required him to be super fit. He had to push himself to the max. He liked the idea of being in a superhero movie because his sons would like it and he rated Louis Leterrier, the director, highly. Tim had actually been interested in being in a superhero movie for a long time but had been waiting for the right part and the right script. He has even admitted that before he played Emil and Abomination that he had been quite jealous of the actors who had been in the X-Men-type roles.

AGENT ZERO

 Appears in: *X-Men Origins: Wolverine* (2009)

 Powers: Ability to absorb kinetic energy for added strength or to fire as blasts at opponents; ability to heal

 First comic-book appearance: February 1992

Agent Zero is one of the mutants in Team X, the group that Lgan and his half brother Victor (Sabretooth)are invited to join by Major William Stryker. Agent Zero is a trained killer who is super fast and a master with firearms. He is able to absorb kinetic energy from an impact and use it to give him super-strength. He completes his missions without fearing what he is about to face and he just does as he is told.

When Wolverine escapes from the Weapon X Facility and goes on the run it is Agent Zero who is given the task of tracking him down. He is a ruthless killing machine and kills the elderly couple who are letting Wolverine stay in their barn. He pursues Wolverine in a helicopter but he is destroyed when the helicopter blows up after Wolverine ignites a trail of fuel with his new adamantium claws.

The actor chosen to play Agent Zero in *X-Men Origins: Wolverine* was Korean Star Daniel Henney. Daniel was offered the part without even having to audition because the casting directors had seen his movie *My Father* and were more than impressed with his acting abilities. Just over a week after they offered him the part he was in New Zealand shooting the film alongside Hugh Jackman and Liev Schreiber.

AZAZEL

Appears in: *X-Men: First Class* (2011)

Powers: Ability to take on human forms and to teleport

First comic-book appearance: October 2003

Azazel is the leader of the Neyaphem. They used to rule earth but now live in another dimension after the Cheyarafim mutants forced them to leave. Azazel wants to rule the earth again.

Azazel is a mutant with demon-like powers and he has had lots of relationships to create his own mutant children. He seduced Mystique, which resulted in her giving birth to Nightcrawler. All of his offspring can teleport and he thinks this will help him in his quest.

The actor chosen to play Azazel in *X-Men: First Class* was Jason Flemyng. The film's producer Bryan Singer told the *Los Angeles Times*: 'I'm also excited about Jason Flemyng as Azazel, which is a really cool character. It's like this sinister alter ego of Nightcrawler in a way, which again brings some of the things that we like about that character but at the same time has a different quality.'

B IS FOR...

BANE

- Appears in: *Batman & Robin* (1995), *The Dark Knight Rises* (2012)
- Powers: Super-strength
- First comic-book appearance: January 1993

In the 1995 movie *Batman & Robin*, Bane was a prisoner who was turned into a huge fighting machine by a mad scientist called Dr Jason Woodrue. He gave Bane the steroid venom that gives him his strength. He wears a special mask with tubes that are filled with venom and pump it into his system all the time.

Bane is the big villain in the new Batman movie *The Dark Knight Rises*, which is scheduled to be released in July 2012. The actor chosen to play him is Tom Hardy. Tom is an English actor who is most famous for playing Eames in the Leonardo DiCaprio film *Inception*.

Christian Bale, who plays Batman in the film, told *Empire* magazine once Tom was cast: 'He [Tom] seems like he's balls-out, doesn't he? Like he really goes for it. He looked like a guy that was happy to go to extremes, to really push it. Looks like he could go the distance…'

Bane is a different villain to the Joker and the Scarecrow. He is physically strong rather than mentally strong. In the comics Bane has broken Batman's back and has been murdering people since he was eight years old. It is not known how much of his original background will be used by the scriptwriters for *The Dark Knight Rises*.

BLACKHEART (LEGION)

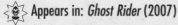 Appears in: *Ghost Rider* (2007)

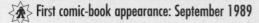 Powers: Super-strength, telekinetic powers, telepathic powers; ability to change his body shape and levitate

First comic-book appearance: September 1989

Blackheart and his father Mephistopheles are the two central villains in the movie *Ghost Rider*. Blackheart is the son of Satan and his pale skin combined with jet-black hair makes him truly terrifying. He might look almost human but once he shows his fangs and reveals his black eyes there's no mistaking his demonic heritage.

In many ways he is more powerful than Mephistopheles because he can enter churches and not be affected. He is able to do this because he was born in Hell, so holy places and things have no affect on him. Ghost Rider's Penance Stare isn't a threat to him either because he doesn't have a soul. When Ghost Rider uses his Penance Stare the person experiences all the hurt and pain they have caused people in the past. It didn't work on Blackheart when he didn't have a soul, but now he has a hundred so experiences 100 times the pain. He is a killing machine and enjoys using his bare hands to kill rather than using the other methods available to him. He can smell the fear in people when he walks by.

When Blackheart turns into Legion his white skin turns blue and his once black eyes turn red. He has called on a thousand cursed souls to enter him, so he can be even more powerful. He might think he's indestructible but he is no match for Johnny Blaze. The Ghost Rider now realises that his Penance Stare is a suitable weapon because of Legion's thousand souls – and quickly uses it against him.

The actor chosen to play Blackheart and Legion was Wes Bentley. He is most famous for playing Ricky Fitts in the film *American Beauty*. Wes really enjoyed his big fight scenes with Nicolas Cage and liked the way Blackheart was portrayed in the movie. In the comics Blackheart was never in human form; instead he was a black-skinned demon with a tail. By playing Blackheart in human form Wes actually made him scarier.

BLOODNOFSKY (CHUDNOFSKY)

 **Appears in:** *The Green Hornet* (2011)

Powers: None but has a two-barrel signature gun

First comic-book appearance: n/a

Chudnofsky is the main bad guy in *The Green Hornet*. The other bad guy is District Attorney Scanlon, but he hides his evil intentions whereas Chudnofsky is happy to show the world that he is the number one gangster in Los Angeles.

Chudnofsky hates it when the *The Daily Sentinel* starts running front-page stories on the Green Hornet, and is furious when his drug business starts getting targeted by the mystery man. He wants the Green Hornet and his sidekick (Kato) out of the picture so he sets up a meeting. He blocks off their escape route and then uses construction vehicles to tip their car into a massive hole and bury them alive. He thinks he has successfully got rid of them but Kato has prepared for every eventuality and blasts them out in no time. Chudnofsky is so angry when one of his henchmen is killed as the pair make their escape that he puts a bounty of one million dollars on the Green Hornet being found dead or alive. Several innocent people end up being murdered as the LA criminal underworld goes on the hunt for anyone wearing green.

Chudnofsky decides that having an evil-sounding name would make him sound scarier, and comes up with the idea of becoming Bloodnofsky, a supervillian who wears a red trench coat. He is working alongside District Attorney Scanlon and between them they control the crime network in Los Angeles. Bloodnofsky contacts the Green Hornet via email offering to give him half of the city if he kills Britt Reid. This is an impossible task because Britt Reid *is* the Green Hornet. He doesn't actually read the message but Kato does. The duo have recently parted ways and Kato wants to be the superhero everyone is talking about instead of the driver/sidekick.

He drives the Green Hornet's car to the Habachi Grill, knowing that District Attorney Scanlon will be inside talking to Britt. As Kato steps out of the car Bloodnofsky asks where the Green Hornet is, but after hearing that he isn't coming and his friend is going to do the hit instead, he has doubts. In the end he lets Kato do the job after seeing how easily he defeats his henchmen. Kato goes inside but instead of killing Britt he helps him escape. Bloodnofsky realises that he has been tricked and that Britt is the Green Hornet. Scanlon gives chase, alongside Bloodnofsky, as Britt has recorded his conversation with the corrupt District Attorney and it would ruin his career if it got out.

The men end up at the headquarters of *The Daily Sentinel* because Britt wants to get the recording made public. He rushes upstairs as Kato tries to fight as many of Bloodnofsky's men as possible. Bloodnofsky stops mid-fight to put on his red costume and gas mask. He ends up fighting with both Kato and the Green Hornet, and for a while it looks like he is going to kill them both before Kato stabs him with a table leg and the Green Hornet shoots him with his own famous two-barrel gun.

The actor who played Bloodnofsky in the movie was Christoph Waltz. He became only the second person in the world to win an Oscar for playing a Nazi in 2010. He won the award for his role in the Quentin Tarantino movie *Inglourious Basterds*. Christoph has played lots of bad guys over the years, but he enjoyed playing a bad guy in a comedy for a change. He loved the fact that Chudnofsky is going through a midlife crisis so decides to become Bloodnofsky.

BULLSEYE

 Appears in: *Daredevil* (2003)

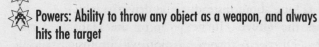 Powers: Ability to throw any object as a weapon, and always hits the target

First comic-book appearance: March 1976

Bullseye is an assassin hired by Kingpin. He can use almost anything as a weapon to kill someone but he prefers to kill by throwing the shurikens concealed in his belt buckle. They are sharpened discs which can easily deliver the killer blow to his victims. When he isn't throwing his shurikens he will happily use pencils, paperclips and shards of glass to kill people. He even used Daredevil's billy club to kill Elektra's father, which made her wrongly think that Daredevil had done it.

He loves being unbeatable so is shocked when Daredevil manages to evade him. He wants to finish the job he started so looks forward to killing him. Elektra meanwhile attacks Daredevil, before realising that Bullseye was her father's killer. She battles with Bullseye, but he is too strong. He picks her up by the throat and then uses her own weapon against her, stabbing her with one of her *sai* (a sharp dagger-like weapon used in martial arts). He throws her from a rooftop, pulls a red nose, the trademark of Kingpin, from his pocket and wipes it on his forehead before throwing it next to her body.

Daredevil arrives too late and has to watch as Elektra passes away. He chases after Bullseye to a church where they fight. Bullseye cleverly uses the bells and parts of the church's organ to distract Daredevil, as he can't cope with loud noises. He is stumped when he runs out of shurikens and ends up breaking a stained glass window so he can use the shards of glass as his weapon. He tosses them at Daredevil but they miss him as he does continuous back flips. They carry on fighting but Daredevil hears a bullet being fired by a SWAT sniper and manages to move Bullseye's arm so that the bullet goes through both of his hands. Bullseye is no match for Daredevil without the ability to throw things, and Daredevil throws him through a window. He lands on journalist Ben Urich's car and it is a miracle that he survives. He ends up stuck in a hospital bed, supposedly unable to move, but he still manages to throw a needle at a fly that is annoying him and kills it.

Bullseye was played by Irish actor Colin Farrell who is most famous for his roles in *Minority Report* and *Phone Booth*. According to the comics Bullseye should wear an all-in-one blue superhero-type costume but the Lycra look was abandoned in favour of leather trousers and a trench coat for the film. The new

Bullseye had a goatee, earrings, tattoos and a bullseye branded on his forehead.

DID YOU KNOW?

Before the film came out, changes were made in the comics to make Bullseye look more like Colin Farrell's interpretation.

Colin enjoyed being able to use his natural Irish accent to play Bullseye as he usually has to put on an American accent in his films. He had a pretty easy make-up routine as well: the bullseye brand on his forehead was made out of gelatine and only took about 10 minutes to stick on every morning, and his costume wasn't anything elaborate. He got off quite lightly compare with the complex make-up and costumes other actors playing supervillains have to wear.

Learning to fight was tricky, though, and Colin had to bring in an expert to teach him the choreography. He told the *Latino Review* about his teacher: 'Cheung-Yan Yuen, the master. He was doing it and not a word of English. You'd have his translator. He does all the wirework, so we did quite a bit of wirework and he choreographed all the fights and helped … he's great. He's a genius. It was quite fun to do. It was quite fun to see that aspect of it. A lot of waiting around though.'

C IS FOR...

CARMINE FALCONE

- Appears in: *Batman Begins* (2005)
- Powers: No superpowers but he controls crime in Gotham
- First comic-book appearance: 1987

Carmine Falcone is an evil man who runs the crime world in Gotham. He has ultimate control, as the police force seems powerless to stop him. He will kill anyone who tries to interfere or threatens to destroy his empire. He arranges for criminal Joe Chill to be killed so he can't testify against him in court but this leads to Bruce Wayne threatening him.

Bruce wanted to see Joe Chill jailed for killing his parents but Falcone robbed him of that. Falcone decides to tell Bruce a few home truths about power and fear, which leads to Bruce going on a journey of discovery around the world. If it wasn't for Falcone he might not have even taken on the role of Batman – but someone has to protect Gotham from men like him.

Falcone isn't content with the power he has and wants more, deciding to work with Dr Jonathan Crane. Together they bring fear toxin into the City – and things are going well until Batman manages to capture him. He wants him to go to prison but Dr Jonathan Crane manages to get Falcone and his men sent to Arkham Asylum instead. Falcone thinks that he can control Crane but the doctor uses the fear toxin on him.

Falcone didn't appear in *The Dark Knight* but it was revealed that he was still a resident of Arkham Asylum.

The actor chosen to play Carmine Falcone was double Oscar nominee Tom Wilkinson. He is best known for his roles in *The Full Monty*, *Shakespeare in Love* and *Eternal Sunshine of the Spotless Mind*.

DID YOU KNOW?

Tom played Britt Reid's dad in *The Green Hornet* (2011). He was murdered by District Attorney Frank Scanlon at the start of the film – but at first everyone thought he'd been killed by a bee sting.

CATWOMAN (SELINA KYLE AND PATIENCE PHILLIPS)

Appears in: *Batman Returns* (1992), *Catwoman* (2004), *The Dark Knight Rises* (2012)

Powers: Superb fighting skills, cat-like flexibility, sharp claws, nine lives

First comic-book appearance: 1940

In her first appearance in *Batman Returns* (1992), Catwoman was played by Michelle Pfeiffer. In this movie Selina Kyle is a lonely secretary and finds out that her boss is planning to steal Gotham's electricity by building a power plant. She didn't want to know her boss's secret but that doesn't stop him trying to kill her. He throws her out of the window to silence her, as she is no threat to him dead.

She lands in the snow and it looks like she's dead, but things change once some stray cats appear and start licking her fingers. She wakes up and makes her way home but she isn't the same Selina any more. She isn't about to let her boss get away with what he tried to do to her and wants revenge. She transforms into Catwoman and joins the Penguin on his quest. She has supernatural powers and she's going to use them to her full advantage.

Because Selina has developed a split personality she stills masquerades as Selina in the daytime and Catwoman at night. Her human side falls for Bruce Wayne and she soon discovers that he is Batman. He too realises that she is the mysterious Catwoman.

At the end of the movie, Catwoman electrocutes her former boss and the explosion it creates causes Batman to think that she has been killed. She hasn't at all, and has instead chosen to slip off into the night.

DID YOU KNOW?

Michelle Pfeiffer actually dated Michael Keaton, who played Batman.

There was going to be a Catwoman stand-alone film starring Michelle Pfeiffer but it was never filmed and instead Catwoman fans had to wait until 2004 to see their heroine on the big screen again. This time she was played by Halle Berry.

The new Catwoman had a new name, Patience Phillips, and a new story arc. She was very different from the Catwoman portrayed in the first movie and in the comic books. She received her supernatural powers from an Egyptian cat goddess and didn't live in Gotham.

To prepare for the role Halle ended up gaining a pet, as she explained to journalist Lena Aburdene: 'If I had to play a dog I'd know how to do it. I adopted a cat and I tried to emulate as many cat-like movements as I possibly could.'

She enjoyed the experience of putting on Catwoman's costume because of the way it made her feel. 'I felt really confident and I felt a difference because everyone reacted to me,' she said. 'Everyone stood back and they were afraid to approach me and when they did, it was with the utmost respect and kindness. It made me feel empowered.'

DID YOU KNOW?

In the film a photo of Michelle Pfeiffer as Catwoman was shown when Patience was looking at photos of the different Catwomen there have been over the course of history.

This film was a big disappointment for fans who had been looking forward to seeing Halle Berry's take on the character. She ended up winning a Razzie award for Worst Actress in a Film. However, instead of snubbing the awards ceremony that gives awards to the worst movies and acting performances of the previous year, she turned up in person. She even brought along the Oscar she had won for *Monster's Ball*. It's amazing really that she could win a Best Actress Oscar and a Razzie for Worst Actress. In her acceptance speech she thanked Warner Brothers for casting her in such a bad movie and even laughed about the acting abilities of Sharon Stone, Benjamin Bratt and the other actors involved. She told the audience watching: 'I'd like to thank the rest of the cast ... to give a really bad performance like mine, you need to have really bad actors.'

Each time Catwoman appears in a movie she is very different, so it will be interesting to see how Anne Hathaway will play her in *The Dark Knight Rises*. She will no doubt be hoping that audiences don't react to her performance in the same way that they reacted to Halle Berry in the role. With Heath Ledger giving such a great performance in *The Dark Knight*, Anne will have her work cut out for her if she wants to make Catwoman as legendary in *The Dark Knight Rises*. The decision has been made for the human part of the character to be called Selina Kyle again, just as she was when Michelle Pfeiffer played her.

D IS FOR...

DEADPOOL (WADE WILSON)

 Appears in: *X-Men Origins: Wolverine* (2009)

 Powers: Incredible array of different powers and abilities taken from other mutants

 First comic-book appearance: 1991

Wade Wilson is a mutant soldier and a walking killing machine. He has two swords that he can move faster than any human, and can even block speeding bullets with ease. His one fault is that he talks too much, and tends to get on the nerves of his teammates.

In *X-Men Origins: Wolverine*, Wade is chosen to become Weapon XI – Deadpool. He is given other mutants' powers so he can be the most powerful mutant of them all. He gets healing powers from Wolverine, Cyclops' optic blasts and John Wraith's ability to teleport. His former Team X comrades had no say in whether Wade would get their powers as they were either kidnapped or murdered by Victor for their powers. Deadpool doesn't have the ability to talk and is controlled by Colonel William Stryker.

In the film's climax he battles with Wolverine and it looks like Deadpool is going to be victorious until Sabretooth returns to help his brother. Wolverine manages to chop off Deadpool's head and it looks like he is dead... although the scene that follows the movie's credits shows Deadpool's hand reaching out for his head.

Canadian actor Ryan Reynolds played Wade Wilson in *X-Men Origins: Wolverine*. He shared the part of Deadpool with Scott Adkins.

When asked about the film's fight scenes by a journalist from Collider.com, Ryan admitted: 'I have a sword sequence in the movie that is no less than a minute long in the film, but that takes months and months to prepare for. When you think about it like that it's vaguely depressing, but when you actually do it, it's worth it. When you see on the screen that it's me and not a stunt person and I'm doing it ... those take a long time but, yeah, they're slow. We had action sequences that took weeks. We had one fight sequence that took weeks to shoot.'

Originally Ryan wasn't going to have much screen time in the movie but this changed. 'Initially it started out as a cameo and they added a little bit more,' Ryan explained. 'For the most part it's definitely Hugh's [Jackman, who plays Wolverine] movie but it also has an ensemble feel. There are a lot of guys in it. There are a lot of characters. They added a bunch of mutants that the fanboys really love.

'I initially jumped in there because I had to shoot *The Proposal* and this other movie called *Paper Man* while they were shooting *Wolverine*, so I was committed to those already when they approached me for the role, so I just said, "Look, if you can make it work, make it work." So we ended up going to do additional photography at the end of *Wolverine* because I still hadn't shot the lion's share of what I was supposed to shoot. So a lot of people thought they were adding scenes because they added more Deadpool, but it was just a function of me finishing the movie that I hadn't completed yet.'

It was thought that Ryan and Scott would both be returning for a Deadpool spin-off movie, but once Ryan signed up to play the Green Lantern many fans thought it wouldn't happen. Deadpool creator Robert Liefeld also had his doubts. He tweeted: 'Warner Bros. just trying to protect their investment. They don't want Ryan Reynolds playing Deadpool AND Green Lantern. Interesting 2 watch.

'Bottom line about Deadpool film is that if FOX doesn't pull the DP film together with Ryan Reynolds between GL films – they should Hari Kari.

'Ryan Reynolds is the new Will Smith, if FOX can't maximise this window of opportunity with this star, this character, that script=MASSV FAIL.

'Hopefully cool heads prevail and are reminded of Harrison Ford and how he played Indiana Jones and Han Solo simultaneously.'

The problem is that *X-Men* and its spin-off movies are under the Fox Studio but *Green Lantern* is under Warner Brothers Studio. Because the studios are rivals they wouldn't want Ryan doing both, and because Warner Brothers Studio is a bigger studio Ryan might want to concentrate on the *Green Lantern*. We'll just have to wait and see what happens but it would be a shame if Ryan Reynolds didn't play Deadpool ever again. He did such an amazing job first time around.

DID YOU KNOW?

Ryan always thought that he was destined to play Deadpool because of something he read in one of the comics. He explained what happened to the *Latino Review*: 'I've always loved the character. I remember reading one of the Deadpool comic books, and somebody asked Deadpool what he looks like. And he said he looks like a cross between a Shar-Pei and Ryan Reynolds. And I was like, I really, really wanna play this guy at some point. I thought it was pretty cool. It's a guy that knows he's in a comic book. How hard is it to shoot that properly? That's not something they put in Wolverine nor would it belong in that universe.'

DOCTOR DOOM (VICTOR VON DOOM)

- Appears in: *Fantastic Four* (2005), *Fantastic Four: Rise of the Silver Surfer* (2007)
- Powers: Sorcery, strength, weapons from his suit; ability to control electricity
- First comic-book appearance: July 1962

Victor Von Doom was the main bad guy in the first Fantastic Four movie, and actually appeared in the second movie, too. Victor is a former classmate of scientist Reed Richards and was in a relationship with Sue Storm when the incident in space occurred.

Victor is a scientific genius and goes with Sue, Reed Richards, Johnny Storm and Ben Grimm in a space shuttle to see some cosmic energy clouds that were due to appear. Reed gets his calculations wrong and the cloud appears a lot sooner than he expected. Ben is on a space walk and is unaware of what is going on so the others leave the shuttle to find him. Victor is the only one who stays behind and he shuts the door to make sure he is safe at least.

The cloud changes Sue, Reed, Johnny and Ben. Sue now has the ability to turn invisible, Reed's limbs become stretchable, Johnny can fly and surround himself in fire and Ben becomes a superhuman rock-like man. Because Victor was inside the shuttle, he doesn't get affected by the cloud like the others and the only change to him is a scar on his face.

When they return to earth Victor is criticised for what happened by his bosses but the other four become heroes and are given the name the Fantastic Four by the media. Victor starts to hate Reed even though he agrees to help him build a machine to try and reverse their changes. Up until this point it seems like the cosmic cloud didn't give Victor any powers but it soon becomes apparent that it did. When Victor gets angry it affects the electricity in the room, and his arm turns to metal. He can control electricity!

Victor doesn't want to use his new abilities for good and instead wants to take his revenge on Reed and the other members of the Fantastic Four. He manages to get Ben and Reed to argue, and then uses Ben's dissatisfaction to help him gain more power. By using the machine to turn Ben back into a human without powers and knocking him unconscious Victor is able to accelerate his own mutation so his whole body turns to metal. He puts on a metal mask and becomes Doctor Doom.

Doom then kidnaps Reed and tries to blow up Johnny, but he manages to outsmart the heat-seeking missile. A powerless Ben can do nothing to help. An invisible Susan tries to free Reed but Doom catches her. They fight but he is too strong. He grabs her by the throat and tosses her on the ground. Just before he can kill her Ben bursts through the wall. He is back being the Thing again as he realised that Sue needed him. He used the machine to give him his powers back. He hits Doom into a metal wall panel and after it falls on him Ben sets about releasing Reed.

Doom hasn't been defeated and takes Ben by surprise. They crash out of the window, fall from a great height, and end up smashing through the roof of a building into a swimming pool, which then causes the ceiling to collapse because of the weight. In the end it takes every member of the Fantastic Four working together to defeat Doom by superheating him and then super cooling him. He ends up a statue, unable to free himself.

In the second movie the Silver Surfer unwittingly releases Doom as he flies past Latveria. The cosmic energy from the Silver Surfer turns Doom from a statue to a human being again. Doom has lost a lot of his power from being a statue for two years so tries to convince the Silver Surfer to join forces with him, but when he refuses and turns to go Doom blasts him in the back. The Silver Surfer quickly hits back, the power of his attack leaving Doom in an ice cave. Doom notices how his hand starts to heal and realises that the power from the blast is healing his whole body.

He contacts the US military and because they want to learn more about the Silver Surfer they agree to his demands. The Fantastic Four are ordered to let Doom work with them. Their mission is to find a way of separating the Silver Surfer from his board because it is from the board that he gets his power. The Fantastic Four and Doom need to stop the Silver Surfer before earth is destroyed as Reed has realised that planets are destroyed after the Silver Surfer has visited them.

Doom builds his own special device secretly which will allow him to control the board. Once the Fantastic Four have separated the Silver Surfer from his board, Doom is able to steal it and become its master. The Fantastic Four come up with a plan to give Johnny all their powers so he can take on Doom. Johnny manages to separate Doom from the board and Ben sends him hurtling into the sea by using a crane.

Doom was played by *Nip/Tuck* actor Julian McMahon in both movies. He loved playing Doom because he was up against a gang of four other people. He thinks it made it a lot more fun than if he had just been fighting one superhero. He used to watch the Fantastic Four cartoons when he was six or seven years old and then he started reading the comics.

During an interview with journalist Rebecca Murray he was asked whether he viewed Dr Doom as a villain or as misunderstood. 'I see him as both,' he told her. 'I see him as both initially – and this is the way we start him off in the movie, and it was really taken from the original comics, like the 56 original comics – and that is that he is a man who is pretty much reasonably egotistical, very much set on getting what he wants out of life and will do whatever he has to do and can do to make sure he gets that. So with that kind of person, that kind of mindset, I think when the circumstances happen to him that happen to him in the movie and everything kind of turns against him, I think it's almost a natural progression for him to go.'

He went on to describe the character: 'He has villainous qualities because he will trample you. I mean, even just as a businessman before he became this Dr Doom thing, he'd run over you if he had to. He didn't care. It was all about business. It was all about making money and getting power. That kind of has a villainous aspect to it to a certain extent, I think, anyway. And then on top of that, I call it the disintegration of a human being. And that's kind of what happens to him in the movie, and also what happens to him in the comics.'

DID YOU KNOW?
Julian McMahon used to be married to Dannii Minogue!

DOCTOR OCTOPUS

Appears in: *Spider-Man 2* (2004)

Powers: Mechanical arms

First comic-book appearance: July 1963

Otto Octavius is a brilliant nuclear scientist and is hired by Harry Osborn to work for Oscorp. He isn't afraid to try new experiments but they don't always end well. When he performed an experiment in sustained fusion his wife was killed and he caused permanent damage to himself. He let a group of scientists watch as he entered his experimental reactor wearing several robotic arms with artificial intelligence. Warning messages flashed up but Otto ignored them. The inhibitor chip which protected his mind from being controlled by the mechanical arms was destroyed. The arms were permanently fused with his spine and Otto changed forever. He becomes Doctor Octopus!

With the mechanical arms now in charge they start killing people that attempt to separate them from Otto. They utilise the worst aspects of Otto's character and make him obsessed with finishing his experiment, whatever the cost. He robs a bank, kidnaps Aunt May and fights Spider-Man.

Harry offers to give Otto the tritium he needs for his experimental reactor if Otto brings him Spider-Man. Otto agrees and tracks down Peter Parker, telling him he wants Spider-Man to meet him at the Westside Tower at 3 o'clock or he will 'peel the flesh' off Mary Jane.

Otto and Spider-Man fight each other all over New York, finally ending up on an elevated train. Otto destroys the brakes and causes the train to travel at maximum speed. He leaves Spider-Man to stop the train and save the passengers, as he knows this will tire him out. Once Peter collapses with exhaustion he takes him to Harry.

Otto heads to the waterfront laboratory with Mary Jane and watches as his reactor starts growing and drawing things into it. Spider-Man arrives and they fight. Otto is extremely strong and his arms make it almost impossible for Spider-Man to attack. Spider-Man gives Otto an electric shock when he breaks the power cables but the reactor still keeps growing. The sudden surge in electricity causes the arms to lose their control over Otto's brain temporarily. Peter convinces him he needs to stop the reactor and when the arms start trying to control him again Otto refuses to let them. He finally takes control and decides to drown the reactor, as it is the only way to stop it. He drowns alongside it.

The actor chosen to play Otto in *Spider-Man 2* was Alfred Molina, a talented actor and producer. He is best known for his roles in *Chocolat*, *The Da Vinci Code* and *Law & Order: Los Angeles* and for producing the TV series *Ladies' Man*, as well as playing the part of Jimmy Stiles. He has been acting professionally since the early 1980's and he played Satipo in *Raiders of the Lost Ark*.

E IS FOR...

ELEKTRA

 Appears in: *Daredevil* (2003) and *Elektra* (2005)

 Powers: Amazing martial-arts skills, limited telepathy, weapons expertise

 First comic-book appearance: January 1981

Elektra is the daughter of billionaire businessman (and criminal partner of the Kingpin) Nikolas Natchios. Her mother was murdered when she was a little girl and since then her father has made sure she can defend herself, just in case she comes under attack. She is a master of martial arts.

In the *Daredevil* film, Elektra's dad is murdered by Bullseye on orders from Kingpin because her dad doesn't want to be involved in crime any more. She is dating Matt Murdock, who is Daredevil, but she doesn't realise this until they battle later on – she wrongly thinks he killed her dad. She fights Bullseye, the real killer, but he stabs her and leaves her for dead. She dies in Daredevil's arms.

In *Elektra*, she has been brought back to life by her martial-arts master Stick. She learns Kimagure (how to control what is going to happen in the future, time, life and death). She doesn't stay with Stick for long because she is still angry about what happened to her and her family. Instead of using her martial-arts training for good she becomes an assassin. She kills for cash.

An anonymous client offers Elektra a lot of money to do a hit but the targets won't be revealed to her until she has been living in the location for a few days. She arrives at her rented base and meets her neighbour Mark and his daughter Abby. They spend time together and soon Elektra starts to have feelings for Mark. When the envelope arrives containing the photos of the people she has to kill she is horrified to see that Mark and Abby are her targets. She attempts to shoot Mark but can't go through with it. She tells her agent that she's decided not to kill them, but he reminds her that the client will just replace her and get someone else to do it.

Elektra decides to stay and protect her new friends. She has to fight numerous assassins from the Hand (an evil ninja group) including Kirigi (the son of the Hand's master). They want to kill Elektra and Mark, and take Abby back with them. Elektra wants Stick to protect Mark and Abby but he wants her to do it. The trio make their way to her agent's house but they are followed.

Elektra senses that they are about to be ambushed so goes with Mark and Abby to the orchard – her agent stays behind to try and buy them some time. He is killed.

Elektra, Mark and Abby fight and kill some of their opponents – Elektra witnesses Abby using martial arts and she is impressed. Evil Typhoid poisons Elektra, but thankfully Stick and his team of ninjas arrive in time to save Elektra, Mark and Abby.

Later, Stick admits to a recovering Elektra that he was the anonymous client who ordered her to kill Mark because he wanted to test her ability to be merciful. He explains that Abby is a martial-arts prodigy and that is why the Hand wanted her. They call her the Treasure.

Elektra knows there is only one way to end it – the Hand will never stop until they have Abby. She confronts Kirigi and suggests they fight, the winner getting Abby. The location of the battle is the home she had when she was a child and where she witnessed her mother being murdered. She had never been able to say who the murderer was but now she realises it was Kirigi. Their fighting is intense, with Kirigi winning. Before he can kill Elektra, Abby appears and she is able to distract him for a few moments so that Elektra can recover.

Elektra and Abby make it outside and head into a maze. Tattoo releases snakes that trap Abby but Elektra kills him. She manages to finally defeat Kirigi by stabbing him, but it looks like all could be lost when Typhoid poisons Abby because he's jealous of her being the Treasure. Elektra kills him and then carries Abby's body inside. She uses the same methods that Stick used to revive her when she was killed by Bullseye, and Abby is able to go back to her dad. By bringing her back from the dead Elektra is officially a Kimagure master.

The actress who played Elektra in both movies was Jennifer Garner – although her official name now is Jennifer Affleck as she is married to *Daredevil* actor Ben Affleck. Jennifer thinks that Elektra is a good role model for young girls as she has brains as well as being beautiful. Her version of Elektra wore a black leather outfit in *Daredevil*, as opposed to the red satin one worn in the comics because of the action scenes in both movies (she would needed the leather padding to protect her from hurting herself). The colour change upset some fans so Jennifer made sure she wore a red outfit in her second film.

Jennifer talked about Elektra's dark side to Cinema

Confidential. She said: 'Elektra is lethal. In *Daredevil* it was somebody who was on the verge of being lethal, who was surprised to find herself vulnerable to someone. Once her father is killed, and this is true in the comic books and in the films as well, there is no life for her in the world any more. I think when she's younger and in college, she kind of had an ideology the same as Matt Murdock's. She feels like she wants to make the world better, and the second her father is killed; everything changes for her.

'Clearly, she almost dies but is resurrected and when Stick kicks her out of the only home that she believes she has left in the world, she uses her skills to become an assassin. That is what she is. She's a mercenary. She is out for blood. She could care less who you are, what you do, where you come from, and I have to say, I love that about her, because I feel like she's been driven to it and she's hiding behind her own soullessness. And she uses it to isolate her completely and emotionally from the world, and physically from the world.'

She also explained that although Elektra is bad, it's about survival: 'This is something that can define her and she's indefinable. At this point she has nothing. She doesn't have her father, she doesn't have her sensei, she doesn't have Matt, so, to me, this particular story is about her not being able to deny her need for her own redemption. And it comes up and smacks her on the face, much like falling for Matt Murdock did. Except I think this is much more of a surprise and it's much more of a twist and it's something that she fights a lot harder than she fought when falling for Matt.'

F IS FOR...

FATHER (DAVID BANNER)

 Appears in: *Hulk* (2003)

 Powers: Highly intelligent, ability to meld with anything he touches, super-strength

 First comic-book appearance: 1985

The major villain in the 2003 *Hulk* movie was David Banner, the father of Bruce. He is mentally unstable and has spent years locked in a mental hospital.

Years ago, David had been a genetic research scientist and blamed himself when his son started to mutate, with green patches of skin appearing whenever he was angry or happy. David had been testing things on himself so felt he was to blame.

He tried to research a cure but General Ross stopped him and this caused him to get so angry that he ended up destroying his lab. He thought that the only solution was to kill Bruce before his mutation went too far and he became a monster. Bruce's mum Edith tried to stop him and ended up being killed herself. With his mum dead and his dad unstable, a young Bruce was put into foster care.

The years pass and David remains in the mental hospital until one day the authorities deem him fit enough to be released. By this time Bruce has started to turn into the Hulk every time someone makes him really angry. David has a feeling that Bruce is his long-lost son and decides to test him. He has given three dogs super-serum so they mutate into gamma dogs, and he sends them out to kill Bruce's love interest Betty Ross, the general's daughter. Bruce ends up being captured by the military.

David experiments with himself after raiding Bruce's lab and gains the ability to meld with anything he touches and ends up fighting the Hulk. He keeps changing appearance as they fight in the sky, on the ground and by the lake. He tries to take some of the Hulk's power, which is a big mistake. He turns into an energy bubble and explodes when General Ross uses a gamma charge bomb. Bruce manages to survive because he is underwater.

In *Hulk* Nick Nolte played the present-day David and Paul Kersey played the younger David in the flashbacks.

DID YOU KNOW?

In the comics Bruce's father is called Brian Banner not David Banner. The name was changed to David in the movie because he was called David in *The Incredible Hulk* TV series, which aired from 1977/8 to 1982.

G IS FOR...

GALACTUS

 Appears in: *Fantastic Four: Rise of the Silver Surfer* (2007)

 Powers: Ability to devour worlds

 First comic-book appearance: March 1966

Galactus is the 'destroyer of worlds' and the Silver Surfer is his servant. He needs to feed off planets, so the Silver Surfer goes ahead of him and finds the planets that have life. The Silver Surfer's board is a homing device that summons Galactus.

Galactus appears as a dark cloud in *Fantastic Four: Rise of the Silver Surfer*. This is not his normal guise, but the director wanted to leave him a bit of a mystery so that he could be explored more in a spin-off Silver Surfer movie. Sadly, this was never made.

GENERAL ZOD (AVRUSKIN)

✦ Appears in: *Superman: The Movie* (1978), *Superman II* (1980)

✦ Powers: Same as Superman

✦ First comic-book appearance: 1961

General Zod is a criminal who was sentenced to a 'living death' in the Phantom Zone by the ruling council of Krypton. His two fellow criminals Ursa and Non were also sent there. They hated Superman's biological father Jor-El because he was the one who provided the evidence that caused them to be condemned.

Many years later, General Zod, Ursa and Non escape the Phantom Zone when Superman detonates a hydrogen bomb in space. They head for Earth with new powers that they have gained from the sun and force the President of the United States to surrender. Earth is now under General Zod's control!

Lex Luthor joins General Zod on his mission as he thinks the Kryptonian might let him control all the real estate in Australia if he can give him Superman. Lex tells them to kidnap Lois, and Superman will soon find them. He does and they are soon battling all over Metropolis. General Zod threatens to hurt the humans around them, knowing that this will upset Superman, as his compassion towards humans is a potential weakness General Zod can exploit.

Superman decides to head for the Fortress of Solitude because they will be alone there. General Zod, Ursa and Non follow him (bringing along Lois and Lex). They think they have outsmarted Superman when they force him to go into the transformation chamber which should strip him of his powers. What they don't realise is that Superman has reversed the process so that he keeps his powers and everyone outside the chamber is exposed to the red light, removing their powers. General Zod, Ursa and Non are then powerless and have no way of attacking Superman.

General Zod was played by Terence Stamp and his line 'kneel before Zod' became a classic superhero movie line.

GLENN TALBOT

Appears in: *Hulk* (2003)

Powers: n/a

First comic-book appearance: 1964

Glenn Talbot was one of the bad guys in the 2003 *Hulk* movie. He used to be in the army but now works in the bioscience field. Glenn is hungry for success and will do whatever it takes for him to be on top. He wants to make a lot of money and even though he has known Betty Ross for a long time that doesn't stop him wanting to take over her science lab, despite her protests.

Glenn recognises that he can become super-rich if he discovers what makes Bruce turn into the Hulk and sets about getting a tissue sample. Bruce manages to escape by turning into the Hulk. Glenn should run for cover but he refuses and tries to shoot a missile at the Hulk. This plan backfires when the missile rebounds off the Hulk and hits him instead. Bye-bye Glenn!

The actor who played Glenn was Josh Lucas. Josh played Reese Witherspoon's love interest in *Sweet Home Alabama* and Dylan Johns in *Poseidon*.

SARAH OLIVER

GREEN GOBLIN (NORMAN OSBORN)

✸ Appears in: *Spider-Man* (2002), *Spider-Man 2* (2004) and *Spider-Man 3* (2007)

✸ Powers: Super-strength, heightened senses, advanced weaponry including goblin glider and pumpkin bombs

✸ First comic-book appearance: July 1964

Norman Osborn is a very rich businessman, being the CEO of his own company Oscorp. He has one son, Harry, and did have a wife but she died when Harry was still a baby. Oscorp is a company that manufactures chemicals.

Norman is very interested in Peter Parker, Harry's best friend and classmate. He sees Peter as a bright young man who has huge potential. In many ways he views Peter as the son he never had and ignores Harry.

Norman wants his company to supply chemical weapons to the US army but this puts him under immense pressure. The army insist that the weapons are tested, so Norman becomes the guinea pig. The drugs give him superhuman strength but they mess with his head, too, leaving him with a split personality. He kills his assistant and several of his rivals before contacting Spider-Man. Wearing an armoured suit and using a goblin glider to get around he becomes the Green Goblin.

The Green Goblin contacts Spider-Man and says he wants them to work together, but when Spider-Man refuses he tries to blackmail him. He discovers that Peter is Spider-Man so attacks Aunt May, almost killing her.

Aunt May ends up in hospital and when Harry tells his dad that he saw Peter hold hands with Mary Jane, Norman knows of another way to attack Spider-Man. The Green Goblin kidnaps

35

Mary Jane and a tram carriage full of school children, dangles them both from the Queensboro bridge and then drops them. He wants to test Spider-Man by seeing who he saves, Mary Jane or the children. Happily Spider-Man manages to save both and then continues his battle with the Green Goblin.

The fighting is intense and it looks like the Green Goblin is going to win until Spider-Man is able to use his web to pull down a wall on top of him. The Green Goblin gloated that he would be going after Mary Jane once he had killed Spider-Man, which made Spider-Man angry enough to launch a counterattack. The Green Goblin tries to distract Spider-Man by revealing that he is Norman, and that the Green Goblin has been controlling him. As he is speaking he is activating his goblin glider behind Spider-Man. Luckily Spider-Man uses his spider sense to estimate when the glider will hit and jumps out of the way at just the right time. The glider flies into the Green Goblin, its sharp spikes ripping into his suit. In his final words he asks Spider-Man to not tell Harry that he was the Green Goblin.

In the second and third movie Norman appears when Harry hallucinates.

DID YOU KNOW?

Jim Carey and Nicolas Cage were both contenders to play the Green Goblin but they turned it down. Willem Dafoe ended up with the job — and he was a great Green Goblin.

Willem Dafoe was so dedicated to the role he played that he insisted on doing the stunts and wearing the Green Goblin's suit even though he could have let a stuntman do it instead. The suit was made up of almost 600 parts. He found getting used to the suit and the glider took time as he explained to Paul Fischer in

Films Inside Out: '[It's] a little more complicated than it looks 'cause the glider is usually used in lots of different ways – sometimes it's on the Gimbal, sometimes on the train, sometimes it's on the insert copy, sometimes it's on wires. And, of course, with all this effects stuff, the shooting ratio is huge. I mean, you can shoot for three days on the glider and you end up having a tiny little sequence in the movie. It's always like that, but particularly with effects work like this.'

He had to practice a lot to get used to the suit. 'I had lots of time to get used to that because it was developed, really, on my body,' he explained. 'They had a design which got very complicated. I mean at one point there was a backpack, with two lights that went on, the phosphorescent effects but they said, "Wow, like this is too much. This is too much going on."'

As well as getting used to wearing the suit he had to learn how to look good fighting in it. He said: 'So it was a long process of fittings and designing the suit for my body which I had to get used to. I played around with the stunt guys in choreographing the fight and we played around with different types of movement. We even worked with this guy Chuck Jeffries in doing some really specific physical stuff, which was very interesting but was too danced and too like a martial art. We needed something to contrast with Tobey's movement that is acrobatic and more fluid. So we ended up with a pretty "meat and potatoes" kick, punch, and stuff.'

H IS FOR...

THE HAND

 Appears in: *Elektra* (2005)

 Powers: Martial arts experts

 First comic-book appearance: January 1981

The Hand is a group of evil ninjas who try to kill Elektra and her friend Matt, and kidnap his daughter Abby. They are assassins and will kill anyone who gets in their way. They are the servants of a demon called the Beast and are feared by people all over the world.

They are led by Roshi and include his son Kirigi and ninjas Kingku, Stone, Tattoo and Typhoid. They are enemies of Stick, Elektra's former martial-arts master, and his Chaste group. Elektra manages to successfully defeat the Hand and saves Abby's life.

HECTOR HAMMOND

⚜ Appears in: *Green Lantern* (2011)

⚜ Powers: Telepathy and incredible intelligence

⚜ First comic-book appearance: April 1961

Dr Hector Hammond is a research scientist who is given the task of examining Abin Sur's dead body. Abin is the Green Arrow who crash-landed and gave Hal his ring. A piece of Parallax remains in Abin's body and causes Hector's brain to mutate when he comes into contact with it.

As his brain swells, Hector gains psychic powers and is able to use telepathy. He is one of Hal's enemies in the movie and was played by Peter Sarsgaard.

DID YOU KNOW?

Peter Sarsgaard is married to Maggie Gyllenhaal who played Rachel Dawes in *The Dark Knight.*

THE HIDDEN

⚜ Appears in: *Ghost Rider* (2007)

⚜ Powers: Various

⚜ First comic-book appearance: n/a

The Hidden are three evil demon spirits that work for Blackheart as he searches for the contract of San Venganza. They also attack Ghost Rider for him. The earth demon is called Gressil and he is the first demon/person Ghost Rider destroys;

the next is Abigor, the air demon. Roxanne and the police force witness Ghost Rider destroying him, which ends up showing Blackheart that Roxanne is Ghost Rider's weak spot. He kidnaps her and tries to force Johnny's hand.

During the climax of the film, when Johnny is on his way to meet Blackheart to exchange the contract for Roxanne's life, he has to face the water demon Wallow who has been sent to slow him down. Wallow has the ability to control water and 'melt' into it. He manages to defeat Wallow and a short time later defeats Blackheart/Legion.

I IS FOR...

IVAN VANKO (WHIPLASH)

 Appears in: *Iron Man 2* (2010)

 Powers: Wears an arc-reactor-powered suit with whip-like weapons

 First comic-book appearance: n/a

Ivan Vanko is grieving for his dad when sees Tony Stark on TV. He is a Russian physicist and hates Tony Stark because Tony's dad betrayed his own dad. Anton Vanko gave up everything to go and work with Tony's dad on the first arc reactor only to get fired and sent back to the Soviet Union. Ivan wants revenge.

He builds his own arc-reactor-powered suit using his dad's blueprints and thinks of the best place to attack Tony...

While Tony is enjoying being in Monte Carlo for the Grand Prix he decides to race himself – to his friend Pepper's horror.

During the race Ivan appears, destroying cars with his whip-like weapons powered by his arc-reactor suit. He attacks Tony's car and if it hasn't been for Pepper and Happy's quick thinking Tony would have been a goner. They drive onto the track, try to run down Ivan and throw Tony the case that transforms into his Iron Man suit. Tony manages to defeat him and Ivan is sent to prison.

Tony's rival Justin Hammer decides that if Tony won't hand over his suit to the US government so he can copy it then he will ask Ivan to help him build one. He helps Ivan escape from prison by faking his death, stupidly thinking that he can outsmart him. He gets Ivan to build military drones using the suit that James provided to the military.

Meanwhile, Justin decides to unveil his drones at the Stark Expo to take the attention away from Tony. Ivan has other ideas. He sends Tony a message telling him he is alive and wants revenge.

At the Expo, Justin introduces the drones and Rhodey in the War Machine suit. Ivan commands them to attack Tony/Iron Man. Rhodey is powerless to stop as Ivan has complete control of his suit. Iron Man quickly flies outside and attempts to escape the drones. Justin gets arrested and Natatalie/Natasha heads to Justin's headquarters with Happy to try and apprehend Ivan. He manages to escape but the duo manage to give Rhodey control over his War Machine suit again.

Once Rhodey's suit becomes under his control again he rushes to the side of Iron Man and they fight together to defeat the remaining drones and Ivan. They might not be able to defeat Ivan individually but together they can by firing repulsor rays at each other. Ivan's suit becomes damaged and without it he is virtually powerless. Once he realises that it is all over for him, Ivan activates the self-destruct device that blows up himself and the drones. The blast destroys the Stark Expo complex but Iron Man and War Machine survive.

The actor who played Ivan was Mickey Rourke. Mickey

revealed to the *Guardian*, 'I decided to do half my role in Russian and that's hard because the Russian language doesn't roll off the English-speaking tongue very easily. I spent three hours a day with a teacher, and after two weeks I know four sentences! Let me see, it's sort of like... "Yezzamee menya ... Yezzamee manya obott ... Er, nemaboootty menya ..."' It means "If someone kills me, don't wake me up, because I'd rather be dead than live in your world."'

He also prepared by visiting a Russian prison and by working out a lot.

DID YOU KNOW?

A lot of the Ivan we see on screen was created by Mickey. He was the one who came up with the idea of Ivan being covered in tattoos, his teeth, his accent and his bird!

J IS FOR...

JIGSAW (BILLY RUSSOTI)

- Appears in: *Punisher: War Zone* (2008)
- Powers: None, but he is athletic and cunning
- First comic-book appearance: November 1976

Billy Russoti got his nickname 'The Beaut' because he was so good-looking. He isn't any more and now goes by the name Jigsaw. He is a sadistic assassin and the Punisher ended up causing permanent damage to his face. His face is so disfigured that it would give you nightmares just looking at it.

The Punisher was killing some criminals at a meeting when Billy escaped so he had to hunt him down. He ended up falling on a glass-crusher machine and the Punisher decided to turn it on. It ground his face and left his facial muscles and tendons beyond repair. He tried to get it fixed by visiting a plastic surgeon, but after getting told it couldn't be fixed he killed the surgeon and decided to go after the Punisher.

He broke his evil and dangerous brother James 'Loony Bin Jim' out of a mental institution to help him and they plot the Punisher's demise. Once they catch up with the Punisher things don't go to plan and Jigsaw ends up being impaled on a pole and thrown into a fire. Loony Bin Jim gets shot in the head by The Punisher.

The actor who played Jigsaw in *Punisher: War Zone* was Dominic West; Loony Bin Jim was played by Doug Hutchison. Dominic describes Billy as going from being the vainest man in the world to the most sadistic man in the world when he becomes Jigsaw.

JOKER

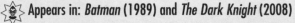 Appears in: *Batman* (1989) and *The Dark Knight* (2008)

Powers: No specific powers although he is highly intelligent and always seems one step ahead of Batman and the authorities

 First comic-book appearance: 1940

In *Batman* the Joker's real name was Jack Napier and he used to work for the gangster Carl Grissom. His face was disfigured when he attempted to shoot Batman and the bullet ricocheted and went through his cheeks. He ended up falling into a container of toxic chemicals and getting washed up in Gotham's harbour. He tried plastic surgery to try and fix his appearance, but this just left him with a permanent grin as the nerves in his face were too damaged.

In this movie the Jack was actually the man who murdered Bruce's parents, and if his sidekick hadn't encouraged him to get a move on he would have killed Bruce as well. Once Jack is disfigured he becomes crazy and wants to become the head of crime in Gotham. He hates the attention Batman is getting from the press and wants people to fear him. He becomes a 'homicidal artist' by killing people with his special Smilex gas, which causes them to die grinning. Batman manages to defeat him by attaching a grappling hook to his leg as he attempts to escape by helicopter. The other end is tied to a stone gargoyle and the Joker ends up hitting the tarmac on the street below when the gargoyle falls. He might be dead but he's still laughing, thanks to a laughing bag in his pocket.

The director of the movie was Tim Burton and he decided to have the Joker die at the end because it would make it more realistic. He didn't want the Joker to come back in the next film. Jack Nicholson played the Joker for the majority of the movie but Hugo E. Blick played Jack in the flashback to Bruce's parents being killed.

In *The Dark Knight* the Joker is a younger man than in the first film, and is portrayed by Australian actor Heath Ledger. He is still a dangerous psychopath but instead of having a perfectly drawn-on clown's face his is smudged and dirty-looking. He is a bank robber who uses criminals to do his dirty work before getting them to kill each other (he kills the last one). His aim is not to create 'killer art' but to use crime to upset social order. He got his grin from someone cutting into both sides of his face, although the person who did it is never revealed. He does, however, come up with different stories to tell ranging from child abuse to self-harm.

The Joker has no morals and forces Batman to choose whether to save Rachel Dawes or Harvey Dent from being blown to smithereens as he has placed them at opposite ends of the city with bombs set to detonate. Batman tells James Gordon and the police to go rescue Harvey and he will rescue Rachel. When he gets to Rachel's address he finds Harvey. He saves Harvey, although his face is disfigured by the blast, but Rachel dies.

The Joker escapes the police station where he was being held and gives Batman another order. He wants Wayne Enterprises' accountant dead within an hour or he will blow up a hospital. Batman can't kill the man and the Joker visits his chosen hospital, speaks to a recovering Harvey Dent, and then calmly walks out of the building wearing a nurse's uniform and using his detonator to set off explosions. He seems disappointed that there haven't been more explosions, but after inspecting his detonator he presses the button a few more times and then the explosions really start. Soon the whole hospital complex is destroyed and the Joker climbs aboard a nearby bus.

As Gotham residents are warned by the Joker that he's going to blow up the city they start evacuating. This is when the Joker stages his biggest test on humanity. He has two ferries, and in each he has rigged 100 barrels to explode if a simple key is turned on a detonator. On one ferry are normal civilians and on the other are inmates from Gotham's prison. They each have the detonator for the other ferry. If they blow the other ferry up they will live. The Joker's message states that they have until midnight to decide, and to make their choice quickly before the other ferry decides.

In the end neither the civilians nor the inmates can bear to turn their keys and sentence others to death. It gets to midnight and the Joker is horrified that his plan hasn't worked. In his pocket he has a spare detonator but before he has chance to use it Batman throws him off the side of the building. He doesn't let him die, though, and saves him just before he hits the tarmac. He leaves the SWAT team to arrest him.

Heath Ledger sadly died before the film came out but the Joker was to be his best performance by a clear mile. He won an Oscar for Best Supporting Actor and his family collected the award for him.

JUGGERNAUT (CAIN MARKO)

⚙ Appears in: *X-Men: The Last Stand* (2006)

⚙ Powers: Superhuman strength, ability to knock down walls with ease

⚙ First comic-book appearance: July 1965

Juggernaut is a super-strong mutant who is extremely fast and can knock down almost anything with his brute strength. He can run through walls and bust through concrete, no problem. He is a member of the Brotherhood Alliance. He wears a metal helmet to stop mental attacks.

While the mutants are fighting on Alcatraz Island he is sent to get Leech, but he fails when he hits his head on an unbreakable wall so hard that it knocks him unconscious.

Former professional footballer turned actor Vinnie Jones played Juggernaut in *X-Men: The Last Stand*.

DID YOU KNOW?
Vinnie once played the bad guy in Westlife's 'Bop Bop Baby' video.

JUSTIN HAMMER

⚙ Appears in: *Iron Man 2* (2010)

⚙ Powers: None

⚙ First comic-book appearance: March 1979

Ivan Vanko might be the main bad guy in *Iron Man 2* but he wouldn't have been able to attack Iron Man with dozens of drones if it wasn't for Justin Hammer.

Justin is Tony's biggest rival and wants to create his own Iron Man-style suits. He is a defence contractor to the US government. He tries to be as cool as Tony but fails miserably. When Congress are concerned about Iron Man's suit and the damage it could do, Justin shows them a video of one of his own prototype suits going wrong (although he doesn't mention that it was one of his). Tony still refuses to hand over his suit or design.

Justin Hammer figures that if Tony won't hand over his suit to the government so he can copy it then he will ask Ivan to help him build one. Ivan is currently in prison after his attack on Tony in Monaco. Justin helps Ivan escape by faking his death, stupidly thinking that he can outsmart him. He gets Ivan to build military drones using the suit that Rhodey provided to the military. Rhodey handed over a Mark II suit after Tony's birthday party fiasco.

Meanwhile, Justin decides to unveil his drones at the Stark Expo to take the attention away from Tony. As he goes on stage he dances, which shows how much he wants the audience to love him and think he's a cool guy. After Justin introduces the drones and Rhodey in the War Machine suit, Ivan commands them to attack Tony/Iron Man using remote control. Iron Man quickly flies outside and attempts to escape the drones. Justin gets arrested for his part in what happened. His desire for power and fame has cost him dearly.

The actor chosen to play Justin was Sam Rockwell.

DID YOU KNOW?

In the Iron Man comics Justin is supposed to be quite a bit older than Tony, and British. The people behind the film decided they wanted a younger, American Justin instead.

K IS FOR...

KINGPIN (WILSON FISK)

Appears in: *Daredevil* (2003)

Powers: Highly intelligent and physically strong

First comic-book appearance: July 1967

Kingpin is a huge guy who runs crime in Los Angeles. Very few people know that businessman Wilson Fisk is the Kingpin and he wants to keep it that way. He started his crime career working for Fallon and was the man who killed Daredevil's dad. He used to leave a red rose as his calling card.

Now the police have started sniffing round trying to find out who Kingpin is he's decided to set Nikolas Natchios up. He wants Bullseye to kill him and then they'll leave enough evidence to make the police believe that he was Kingpin.

Bullseye kills Nikolas, and after failing to kill his daughter Elektrathe first time he manages it. He then fights Daredevil but is defeated. During their fight he tells Daredevil who the real Kingpin is and that he was his dad's murderer.

Kingpin hears about Bullseye ending up being stretchered into an ambulance and knows that it will only be a matter of time before Daredevil arrives. He prepares himself but is disappointed when Daredevil turns up injured. Kingpin is by far the better fighter and unmasks his opponent, only to find that he is the blind lawyer. He thinks he has won but Daredevil manages to smash the water pipe that runs throughout the office, giving him his 'sight' back. He attacks and manages to break Kingpin's legs.

They hear police sirens and Daredevil explains that they are coming for Wilson – they know he is the Kingpin and he will be going to prison for a long time.

Kingpin was played by the *Green Mile* actor Michael Clarke Duncan. He had to put on almost three stones to play the part, which was quite a challenge. Kingpin was a tough guy so Michael had to spend a lot of time working out to make sure that he wasn't just heavier but more muscular, too.

L IS FOR...

LEX LUTHOR

- Appears in: *Superman: The Movie* (1978), *Superman II* (1981), *Superman IV: The Quest for Peace* (1987), *Superman Returns* (2006)

- Powers: None but is extremely intelligent and possesses kryptonite

- First comic-book appearance: April 1940

In *Superman: The Movie*, Lex is a man obsessed with money and will do whatever it takes to make himself rich. He has his own lair and wears wigs to hide his baldness. His wants to use a nuclear missile to cause California to sink below the water level so that he can make money from his real estate. He is helped by the clueless Otis and his girlfriend Eve Teschmacher, but thankfully Superman stops him and Lex is sent to jail.

In *Superman II* Lex escapes from jail thanks to his girlfriend. He joins up with General Zod because he hopes the Kryptonian will give him all the real estate in Australia once he defeats Superman and rules Earth. Lex doesn't get his wish and ends up back in jail once General Zod loses his powers in the Fortress of Solitude.

In *Superman IV: The Quest for Peace*, Lex's nephew helps him escape from jail. He sets about creating a clone using a strand of Superman's hair and his own DNA. The clone is called Nuclear Man and although he seems powerful to start with he is soon defeated by Superman once it gets dark, as Nuclear Man relies on sunlight for his power. Again, Superman takes Lex back to jail.

In this film, Lex had been sent to prison by Superman but after serving his time has been released. Five years have passed since Superman was last seen on Earth. Lex wants revenge but needs money; he marries a rich widow and sets about creating his own continent so that he can make an even bigger fortune. He makes it out of Kryptonian crystals stolen from the Fortress of Solitude but adds Kryptonite to it so that Superman will be powerless there and will be easier to kill. His continent will cause billions of people to die because it will raise sea levels worldwide, but he doesn't care.

He captures Lois and her son Jason and takes them in his ship to where his landmass is forming. He suspects that Jason could be Superman's son but Lois insists he's her fiancé Richard's son. Jason manages to stop one of Lex's henchmen from hurting his mum by shoving a piano at him. No normal boy would be able to do that. Richard arrives by seaplane to rescue them while Superman heads for the continent to get Lex.

Superman is weakened by the Kryptonite and Lex manages to stab him with a piece of it. He ends up falling into the water but thankfully Richard and Lois arrive and Lois is able to remove it from his back. He quickly recovers and then comes up with an idea. He covers the landmass with soil so that he can pick it up without coming into contact with the Kryptonite and launches it into space. As for Lex, he thinks he has managed to escape but when his helicopter runs out of fuel he is left stranded on a desert island.

The part of Lex Luthor was played by Gene Hackman in *Superman: The Movie*, *Superman II* and *Superman IV: The Quest for Peace*. He was played by Kevin Spacey in the 2006 movie *Superman Returns*.

Kevin Spacey would love to play Lex Luthor in the rebooted *Superman: Man of Steel* but he doesn't think he's going to be asked back because the filmmakers are likely to be looking for new actors.

LIZARD (DR CURT CONNORS)

Appears in: *Spider-Man 2* (2004), *Spider-Man 3* (2007), *The Amazing Spider-Man* (2012)

Powers: Ability to scale walls, a tail he can use to strike his enemies, enhanced healing abilities; he also possesses many of the same abilities as Spider-Man

First comic-book appearance: November 1963

Dr Curt Connors is a physics lecturer at Columbia University and teachers Peter Parker. He believes he's very gifted but thinks he can be lazy at times. Dr Connors has only one arm and was a good friend of Otto Octavius before he turned into Doctor Octopus.

Peter trusts Dr Connors and he takes a sample of the symbiote on his suit to him to try and find out what it is. He runs tests on it and finds out that it changes anyone it comes into contact with by making them more aggressive.

In *The Amazing Spider-Man* movie Dr Connors turns into one of Spider-Man's all-time worst enemies, the Lizard. The actor chosen to play him is Rhys Ifans. It is thought that the Lizard will create clones of himself to make things even tougher for Spider-Man.

LOKI

✴ Appears in: *Thor* (2011) and *The Avengers* (2012)

✴ Powers: He is a sorcerer and a shape-shifter

✴ First comic-book appearance: 1949

Loki is Thor's biggest rival and his adopted brother. Thor's dad Odin found him after killing the King of the Frost Giants, Laufey. Loki was Laufey's secret son as he had been ashamed of how small his son was. Odin was impressed with the strength Loki showed and decided to take him back with him. That is how he became the adopted brother of Thor.

Loki resented his brother from a young age because of the way others treated them differently. They approved of Thor's strength and bravery in battles but dismissed Loki because he wasn't able to do everything Thor could. Instead Loki's strengths lay in sorcery. Now Loki's anger has grown and all he wants is power and revenge. He hates Thor with a passion and vows to destroy mankind.

The actor Tom Hiddleston was chosen to play Loki in *Thor* and *The Avengers*. Tom is an English actor and Loki will be his biggest role to date. He actually auditioned to play Thor at first but was offered the part of Loki instead.

Tom thinks Loki is a great character to play and told Total Film: 'Loki's like a comic book version of Edmund in *King Lear*, but nastier. Loki's skilled in black magic and sorcery. He's a shape-shifter and has all sorts of super powers from the dark arts. He can turn clouds into dragons, things like that.'

He found being in a film with very experienced actors like Anthony Hopkins, Natalie Portman and less well-known actors interesting. He didn't have to work out as much as Chris Hemsworth who was playing Thor because he was supposed to look physically weaker. The director wanted him to look almost 'hungry'.

Tom discussed how he approached the villainous aspects of his character with MoviesOnline. 'Ken [Branagh, the director] and I discussed a lot very early on because we both read a lot of the comics and there were so many facets of him in the comics,' he told them. 'There was kind of an agent of chaos who would go down to Earth and turn whales into sea serpents and plows into dragons and whole streets of cars in New York into ice cream. But then there was also this damaged brother, this younger brother who didn't receive as much love as his elder brother and who was passed over, rejected, betrayed, and I think that became really interesting for both of us actually.'

He went on to describe what they wanted from the character: 'Ken and I suddenly decided we wanted to root all of his mischief in a truthful, psychological damage. He essentially was the younger brother. He was never going to be king and he wished that he could, so all of his stuff comes from wanting to please his father, although there's a big reveal about who his father really is in the course of the film which I won't reveal. But it was rooted in that. I found the duality of that … he's a villain, he has a lot of fun, he's a mischievous prankster but at the same time he's in deep, deep pain.'

M IS FOR...

Magneto (Erik Lehsherr)

✦ Appears in: *X-Men* (2000), *X2* (2003), *X-Men: The Last Stand* (2006) and *X-Men: First Class* (2011)

✦ Powers: He can manipulate metal and has control over magnetism, and all other forms of electromagnetic energy

✦ First comic-book appearance: September 1963

Magneto is the main villain in the X-Men movies. He thinks mutants are superior and wants them to prosper over the weaker humans. He objects to Xavier's (Professor X's) way of thinking and they often clash – with his Brotherhood taking on Xavier's X-Men. He doesn't care who dies and will sacrifice his own mutants if it means he will get what he wants.

Magneto wears a special helmet which stops mutants being

able to read his mind and influence him that way. He was one of the creators of Xavier's Cerebro and this helped him come up with a way of defending himself against it.

In the first film we get to see how a young Magneto manifested his powers for the first time. Nazi soldiers had separated him from his Jewish parents and he twisted open a fence using his powers. After surviving the Holocaust, Magneto was determined that mutants would not be made to feel inferior like the Jews. As a leader of the Brotherhood, Magneto wants to make Senator Kelly change his views on mutants. Kelly wants to bring in a Mutant Registration Act, which involves mutants having to reveal themselves and their powers. Magneto decides to use a machine on Kelly that causes him to become a mutant. Kelly manages to escape by using his new powers and heads for Xavier's school but he dissolves – his human body cannot cope with the change.

Magneto needs someone to be the power source for the machine but doesn't want to risk his own life. He kidnaps Rogue but Wolverine, Cyclops, Storm and Jean soon mount a rescue mission. They fight Magneto's mutants and manage to reach Rogue just in time. Cyclops takes on Magneto, injuring him, which allows Wolverine to destroy the machine and save Rogue who is close to death. He puts his hand on her face and she is able to use her powers to transfer his healing abilities.

Magneto is taken to a plastic prison cell, which stops him being able to use his powers. He plays a game of chess with Xavier, and Magneto warns that he will not stop fighting.

In the second movie, X2, Magneto escapes from prison and joins with Xavier as they fight against William Stryker. He wants all mutants killed and ends up kidnapping Xavier so he can build another Cerebro-type machine at Alkali Lake. Magneto finds out that Stryker has been experimenting on mutants, which makes him very angry. They find out where Stryker is and head there. Once they infiltrate the base Magneto has Mystique take the form of Stryker and tell his son to make Xavier locate and kill humans instead. They think their plan has worked as they leave in a helicopter, but Storm creates a snowstorm which helps Xavier think clearly and reject the messages Jason is putting in his head.

In *X-Men: The Last Stand* Magneto is more powerful and his Brotherhood is much larger as more and more mutants join him after they find out about the mutant cure. Magneto tells mutants that the cure will be used to exterminate them even though it is being promoted as a choice. He manages to recruit the extremely powerful Phoenix (Jean Grey). He had to win her over first, as Xavier tried to convince her to let him help her control her powers. She became angry when he mentioned that she killed Cyclops because she couldn't control her powers and killed him by lifting him out of his wheelchair and lifting up the house they were in; she broke him down into molecules until there was nothing left. Magneto objected because he didn't want Xavier to die but he wanted the Phoenix to join him because she has unimaginable powers, and he left with her.

Magneto and his army head to the Worthington Labs where the cure is being made with the intention of killing a mutant called Leech because he is the cure's source. If he is exterminated the pharmaceutical company wouldn't be able to make any more. They want to destroy the labs, too, which will send a message out that they will destroy anyone and anything that tries to destroy or control them. The X-Men arrive to try and stop him and during the battle the Beast manages to inject Magneto with the cure, turning him into a normal, powerless man.

Later, as Magneto is seen playing chess, he is able to move one piece a fraction without using his hands, which suggests the cure was only temporary and that with time he could become a mutant again and have the same powers.

The actor who played Magneto in the first three X-Men movies was Sir Ian McKellen. He has played some huge roles over his long acting career but the two he is most famous for playing are Gandalf in the *The Lord of the Rings* and Magneto in the *X-Men* movies.

IndieLondon asked Ian during an interview what effect *X-Men* has had on his career. He replied: 'It's given me an immense amount of street cred. On the day after 9/11, I was walking through the smoke and the smells of New York. There were knots of policemen everywhere. As I went past one officer, he called out: "Hi, Magneto." That's an indication of *X-Men's* extraordinary reach. Rather gratifyingly, Magneto in the *X-Men* comic now has a look of Ian McKellen about him!'

He also talked about his friendship with Patrick Stewart who plays Xavier: 'Patrick and I completely bonded. It's odd – although we're both English and have done a lot of theatre, we've only ever worked together in Vancouver. When we first met, he was still feeling an exile in LA. He loved to hear my stories about London, just as I loved to hear his stories about Hollywood. We're so close, we're the same person really!'

A spin-off film telling the story of Magneto's origins was planned but never made. *X-Men: First Class* will instead show how Erik Lensherr turned into Magneto and will have Michael Fassbender taking over the role from Sir Ian McKellen.

MEPHISTOPHELES

 Appears in: *Ghost Rider* (2007)

 Powers: Immortality, unimaginable strength, the ability to own souls, cause people to die and change shape ... and many others

 First comic-book appearance: December 1968

Mephistopheles is the Devil and tricks Johnny Blaze into giving him his soul in return for his dad's cancer disappearing. He passes

Johnny the contract and before he has the chance to sign anything he cuts his finger and his blood seals the deal. He takes on a human form but his shadow reveals the real Mephistopheles – a horned demon.

He wants Johnny to be his Ghost Rider and lets him carry on with his life until summoning him to capture his son Blackheart who wants to become more powerful than him by gaining the thousand souls of San Venganza. He wants to become the ruler of Hell.

Although Johnny does his bidding, and Mephistopheles offers to give him his soul back, he refuses and vows to use his powers against Mephistopheles.

MR FREEZE (VICTOR FRIES)

 Appears in: *Batman & Robin* (1997)

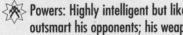 Powers: Highly intelligent but likes to use brute force rather than outsmart his opponents; his weapon of choice is his freeze gun

 First comic-book appearance: February 1959

Mr Freeze is the main bad guy in the *Batman & Robin* movie. He became Mr Freeze after falling into a container of liquid nitrogen while trying to find a cure for the terminal illness MacGregor's Syndrome. His wife was dying from the condition so he put her in a cryogenic chamber until he could cure her. From that day on he has had to wear a special suit, which is powered by diamonds and keeps his body at a very low temperature. The suit also gives him super-strength.

Mr Freeze joins up with Poison Ivy and sets about freezing Gotham until Batman, Robin and Batgirl arrive. Mr Freeze fights Batman until Batman shows him a recording that reveals Poison Ivy saying that she killed his wife Nora. She had been sent to save her and had turned off the chamber instead, but thankfully Batman had arrived in time and reassures Mr Freeze that she isn't dead after all. Ivy had told Mr Freeze previously that Batman had killed his wife and that is why he decided to freeze the city in the first place.

Mr Freeze decides to give Batman the cure he had found for the first stage of MacGregor's Syndrome so that he can save Alfred's (Bruce Wayne's butler's) life. Mr Freeze will continue to search for a cure for advanced MacGregor's Syndrome whilst locked up in Arkham Asylum with Ivy.

The actor chosen to play Mr Freeze was Arnold Schwarzenegger. It took six hours each day to apply his makeup and for him to put on his complex costume.

DID YOU KNOW?

Patrick Stewart, who plays Xavier in the X-Men movies was originally considered for the role.

MULTIPLE MAN (JAMES MADROX)

 Appears in: *X-Men: The Last Stand* (2006)

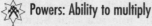 Powers: Ability to multiply

First comic-book appearance: October 1974

James Madrox is a mutant whose special ability is that he can create multiple versions of himself. He uses this ability to rob seven banks at the same time. He is a member of Magneto's Brotherhood and they use him to fool the US army into thinking that the multiple versions of him are them, which means they can sneak off undetected.

The actor who played Multiple Man in *X-Men: The Last Stand* was Eric Dane.

MYSTIQUE (RAVEN DARKHOLME)

Appears in: *X-Men* (2000), *X2* (2003), *X-Men: The Last Stand* (2006) and *X-Men: First Class* (2011)

Powers: She is a shape-shifter

First comic-book appearance: April 1978

Mystique is a mutant who works for Magneto. She has scaly blue skin, yellow reptile-like eyes end combed-back red hair. She is able to change herself into any human or mutant she wants and regularly uses it to trick people into doing what Magneto wants. She walks around naked but can make her skin change to look like she's wearing clothes. She is very flexible and can bend herself out of most tricky situations.

She is devastated to be hit by a mutant cure dart while trying to protect Magneto. She turns into a naked human and Magneto just leaves her as she is of no interest to him without her mutant powers. It is thought that the cure is only temporary, so Mystique could soon be by his side again.

Mystique was played by Dutch-American actress Rebecca Romijn in the first three films but the role was split between actresses Jennifer Lawrence and Morgan Lily in *X-Men: First Class*.

DID YOU KNOW?

When the first movie was being made it could take Rebecca up to ten hours to get into her costume and the fumes from the makeup made her feel sick. In the second film it took her eight hours and in *X-Men: The Last Stand* 3½ hours.

N IS FOR...

NAMOR

 Appears in: *The Marvel Superheroes* TV series

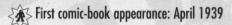 Powers: Amphibious, super-strength, can communicate with sea life, has wings on ankles that allow him to fly

First comic-book appearance: April 1939

Namor is the ruler of Atlantis. His mother was an Atlantean princess and his dad was a US sea captain. He always hated humans when he was growing up but helped them during the Second World War. Once when he was on the surface a man called Destiny took his memory and so Namor ended up living in New York, not knowing who he was. Johnny Storm managed to give him back his memory but by the time Namor returned home Atlantis had been destroyed. This left Namor even angrier with the human race and he fought against the Fantastic Four.

O IS FOR...

OBADIAH STANE

 Appears in: Iron Man (2008)

 Powers: None but when wearing his arc-reactor suit he is virtually unstoppable

 First comic-book appearance: November 1985

Obadiah Stane has been running Stark Industries alongside Tony Stark for many years. He had nurtured Tony and used to work for his dad. Tony thinks he is loyal to him until he discovers that Obadiah wants to take the company away from him because Tony no longer wants to be a weapons manufacturer. Obadiah does this by getting an injunction so that Tony can't even enter his own headquarters any more.

Pepper Potts discovers that Obadiah had organised for Tony to get killed by terrorists in Afghanistan but the terrorists had decided that Tony was more use to them alive. He is hungry for power and gets engineers to build him a suit that is larger and more advanced than Tony's Iron Man suit. He wants his suit to become a new weapon that he can manufacture and make lots of money. In order for his suit to work he steals Tony's arc reactor from his chest, not caring that his actions will kill Tony.

Pepper alerts Agent Coulson from S.H.I.E.L.D. to what Obadiah has been up to and they go to arrest him. He isn't prepared to come peacefully. Thankfully Tony arrives as Iron Man after Rhodey helped him insert his original arc reactor. Obadiah is stronger because he has the newer arc reactor but Tony cleverly draws him onto the roof. His suit can cope with the icy conditions on the roof but Obadiah's can't and Tony tells Pepper to overload the full-sized arc reactor at them. The electrical surge that is generated knocks Obadiah out and sends him through the roof. He lands on the arc reactor and it kills him. Pepper thinks that Tony might be dead, too, because of what she has done, but he manages to survive because he rolled over at just the right time.

The next day the press are told that Obadiah died in a plane crash on holiday. The S.H.I.E.L.D. agents don't want what really happened to get out.

The actor chosen to play Obadiah was Jeff Bridges. Jeff told *Cinecon.com* about the improvisation that he had to do: 'Well, we had some great writers on the set and we had a script that was constantly changing because they were some unusual elements that had to be approved and there was a lot of uncertainty of all that – which drove me crazy at the beginning because I could be prepared as I can and then you read a script and what you said about people and what other people said about you, that's how you define your character, and if that's all up for grabs and nobody's on the same page, you start to panic.

'Often, we would show up for the day's work not knowing what we were going to say for that day. You would go into Jon's [Favreau, the director] trailer for a couple of hours with one of these little tape recorders and we would jam. We would play each other's character and we would all have ideas and throw them around and the writers would be in the room and the producers, and it took me a while to get behind that.

'For a few weeks, I was panicking and it really rubbed my fur the wrong way. That's not how I like to work. However, that's the way to do it. There's certain ways you would like it and it's weird, but that's how it is. It's like you go to a ballroom, and you're all prepare to dance the waltz, and then they just play cha-cha all the time. So, I finally got my cha-cha shoes out, and had fun playing the game that was being played. When I finally got with the program, it was kind of fun and the fact that Jon Favreau is a wonderful actor himself and knows how different actors approach the material and he tried to give us all what we needed and was calm and allowed the way it was to turn into this movie. That's because of Jon.'

OMEGAS

 Appears in: *X-Men: The Last Stand* (2006)

 Powers: Various

 First comic-book appearance: Various

The Omegas are a group of mutants who join with Magneto and his Brotherhood when they attack the pharmaceutical company on Alcatraz Island. They want Leech, the source of the cure, dead, too.

Their leader Callisto is a mutant whose past is unknown and she has the ability to sense the powers of her opponents, locate them and to move super-fast. She hates Storm and as they battle she is electrocuted by her. The comic-book version of the character had an eye patch and lots of scars but the film version has tattoos and a chin piercing.

The other members of the Omegas are Arclight, Kid Omega and Psylocke.

P IS FOR...

PENGUIN (OSWALD COBBLEPOT)

 Appears in: *Batman Returns* (1992)

 Powers: Has his own penguin army but prefers to run away rather than fight when things look tough

 First comic-book appearance: December 1941

The Penguin was born disfigured and his horrified parents tried to kill him by throwing him into the sewers. He didn't die but grew up in the sewers underneath the zoo where he interacted with the penguins. When he was old enough he joined a circus freak show and it's thought that he murdered children who visited.

He is the main villain in *Batman Returns*. The Penguin is bald with the remaining strands of his hair long and greasy; his hands are flipper-like and green liquid drips from his mouth and nose. He wears a top hat and carries a monocle. He wants to be Mayor of Gotham and tries to frame Batman for murder. His big ambition in life is to kill all of the firstborn sons of Gotham and he sends out his clowns to kidnap the children so he can drown them. Batman stops him, so the Penguin orders his penguin friends to take missiles and destroy Gotham.

The Penguin and Batman fight and after falling through a skylight the Penguin ends up in contaminated water. He manages to climb out but the toxic waste has entered his system and he collapses. His penguin friends take his body back to the water.

Danny DeVito played the Penguin in the film. The part was written for him before he was even cast because the scriptwriter thought he would be the perfect Penguin.

POISON IVY (PAMELA ISLEY)

 Appears in: *Batman & Robin* (1997)

 Powers: Ability to intoxicate men and kill them with a kiss; she controls plants and they do her bidding

 First comic-book appearance: June 1966

Poison Ivy is an enemy of Bruce Wayne and Batman. She is a gorgeous woman with long red hair and stunning eyes. She wears outfits inspired by her love of plants.

As a matter of fact, Poison Ivy cares more about plants than she does people. She will do whatever it takes to protect them and wants to replace humans with special plants she has created. She used to be a shy research scientist called Pamela Isley but changed into Poison Ivy when her corrupt boss tried to kill her by knocking her into a shelf filled with dangerous chemicals. The plant chemicals combined with her human body and Poison Ivy was born. The first person she killed was her boss, with a kiss from her poisonous lips. As she attempts to change Gotham into an eco-friendly haven she is helped by her henchman Bane and later joins up with Mr Freeze.

The pheromones that she emits cause the men around her to desire her and fight among themselves; even Batman and Robin are affected. Only Batgirl isn't affected and after battling Ivy manages to defeat her. She ends up stuck in a cell with Mr Freeze in Arkham Asylum with no chance of being released.

Uma Thurman played Poison Ivy and she later went on to play the superhero G-Girl in the comedy *My Super Ex-Girlfriend* (2006). Her character gets dumped and then goes crazy as she tries to make her ex pay. It didn't receive good reviews but Uma was praised.

PRINCE NUADA

 Appears in: *Hellboy II: The Golden Army* (2008)

 Powers: Martial-arts expert

 First comic-book appearance: n/a

Prince Nuada is the main bad guy in the second Hellboy movie. He is searching for three pieces of a crown to give him ultimate power over the Golden Army. He hates humans and wants to destroy them. He doesn't care who he kills to get the pieces, even killing his own father to get his hands on the second piece. His sister goes on the run with the third and final piece.

The B.P.R.D. (Bureau for Paranormal Research and Defence) step in to protect Nuada's sister Nuala – and Abe Sapien falls in love with her. Hellboy defeats a forest god and troll who attacked Nuala on behalf of her brother. Nuada arrives at the headquarters and manages to kidnap his sister and mortally wounds Hellboy. His friends take him to the Angel of Death who saves him after Liz begs. She tells him he going to be a dad, giving him something to fight for.

Abe hands over the final piece of the crown to save Nuala, which allows Nuada control over the Golden Army. Hellboy challenges him to a battle and Nuada has to accept because he is a member of Hell's royalty. They fight and when it looks like Hellboy could be defeated Nuala kills herself, which in turn causes Nuada to feel her pain as they share a special bond. They both die and turn to stone.

Prince Nuada was played by Luke Goss and Princess Nuala was played by Anna Walton. Luke had previously played the vampire Jared Nomak in *Blade II*.

PYRO (JOHN ALLERDYCE)

 Appears in: *X-Men* (2000), *X2* (2003), *X-Men: The Last Stand* (2006)

 Powers: Ability to control fire

 First comic-book appearance: January 1981

Pyro is a mutant who specialises in fire. To begin with he carries a lighter on his person so he can have access to fire at all times and can form fireballs. After he transfers to Magneto's Brotherhood he starts to wear a gadget on his wrist that produces fire whenever he presses a button.

Pyro was a good friend of Rogue and Iceman when he studied at Xavier's school. Not much is known about his past apart from the fact that he grew up in a dysfunctional home. Magneto persuades him to leave Xavier and his friends behind him and join the Brotherhood of Mutants instead. He changes a lot and even fights his old friend during the attack on Worthington Labs.

Iceman manages to end the fight by turning himself into ice and freezing his friend's hands so he can't use them against him. He is then able to knock him unconscious.

In the film what happens to Pyro next is not known but the novel of the movie explains how Iceman carried him to safety before the buildings collapsed.

Pyro was played by Alex Burton in the first movie before Aaron Stanford took over for *X2* and *X-Men: The Last Stand*.

Q IS FOR...

QUEEN OF FABLES

- To date there have been no appearances of the Queen of Fables in a TV show or film
- Powers: Can make monsters from storybooks come to life
- First comic-book appearance: November 2000

The Queen of Fables is a villain who was sent to earth from another dimension hundreds of years ago. She was imprisoned in a storybook but escaped to run amok in New York. She attacked Wonder Woman because of her resemblance to Snow White, the Queen of Fables' former enemy. She used storybook monsters to fight the Justice League of America and turned Manhattan Island into an enchanted forest.

R IS FOR...

RA'S AL GHUL (HENRI DUCARD)

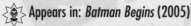 Appears in: *Batman Begins* (2005)

Powers: Long life (he has been alive for hundreds of years), martial-arts and combat expertise, healing abilities

First comic-book appearance: June 1971

Ra's al Ghul is Batman's biggest enemy in the movie *Batman Begins*. He is the leader of the League of Shadows who believe that crime isn't acceptable and that people should lose their lives if they commit a crime.

He is the silent partner of the Scarecrow and Carmine Falcone. The three men plan to destroy Gotham by contaminating the water supply with fear gas.

Bruce Wayne knows Ra's al Ghul as Henri Ducard, a man

who mentored him when he was travelling the world. Henri taught him first of all how to confront his anger and secondly to fight using martial arts, and had another man pretend to be Ra's al Ghul. The League of Shadows wanted Bruce to lead them as they destroy Gotham, but Bruce refuses because he doesn't view Gotham as being all-evil. Bruce ends up battling the pretend Ra's al Ghul and as they fight the temple around them burns. The imposter dies under rubble as Bruce escapes, saving Henri.

Many years pass but at Bruce's birthday party Henri turns up and reveals that he is the real Ra's al Ghul. He also states his intentions for the corrupt city before his men attack Bruce and destroy his home. He organises for the inmates of Arkham Asylum to be released on the streets as the fear gas enters the water supply. As the murderers run riot the police try to catch them but the gas takes over everyone and they start imagining their worst nightmares.

Batman knows he has to save the city from Ra's al Ghul and they battle on board a train that is hurtling towards Wayne Tower. Ra's al Ghul knows that the main water supplies run under Wayne Tower and that if he manages to contaminate the water there, he will have won and Gotham will be destroyed. As Batman fights him Sergeant Gordon is travelling in his Batmobile. He uses the vehicle's weapons to blast the supporting posts holding the train tracks in the air.

Ra's al Ghul mistakenly thinks that Batman wants to stop the train but Batman reveals that he wants the train to keep on going. He manages to overpower Ra's al Ghul just before the section that Gordon has destroyed. Ra's al Ghul wants Batman to kill him but he won't; he just says he won't save him and leaves, flying away on his memory cloth cape. Ra's al Ghul has to watch helplessly as the train falls and crashes to the ground below.

The roles of Henri Ducard and the real Ra's al Ghul were played by Liam Neeson. The fake Ra's al Ghul was played by Ken Watana.

RASPUTIN

Appears in: *Hellboy* (2004)

Powers: Occult abilities and ability to be resurrected

First comic-book appearance: February 1992

Rasputin is the main bad guy in the first Hellboy film. His full name is Grigori Efimovich Rasputin and he is an evil man with occult abilities. He works alongside the Nazis as they open up a portal to another dimension in the hope that they can free the Ogdru Jahad. They are the Dragons of Revelation and Rasputin believes they will destroy the world and form a new paradise. The Allies send in a team to stop this happening and they succeed in destroying the portal, although two key Nazis escape. Rasputin is swallowed up by the portal but a demon baby makes it through; they call him Hellboy.

Sixty years pass, and Rasputin's Nazi friends decide to resurrect him. The B.P.R.D. (Bureau for Paranormal Research and Defence) are tasked with trying to stop him once and for all. Rasputin, Kroenen and Haupstein unleash a monster called Sammael who is given the power of reincarnation. Each time he is killed he multiplies, which makes him one tough opponent for Hellboy and his team. Liz unintentionally knocks herself, Hellboy and Jon out for the count when she uses her powers and Rasputin seizes them. He tries to force Hellboy to become the Ogdru Jahad (his real identity) by sucking out Liz's soul and says he will only let her have it back if Hellboy does as he wishes. Hellboy decides to do it but John manages to talk him out of it by telling him he can control his own destiny. Hellboy rips off his Ogdru Jahad horns and stabs Rasputin. This creates an even bigger problem because Rasputin's body opens to reveal the monster Behemoth. Hellboy lets himself get swallowed by Behemoth but sets off hand grenades which destroy the monster from the inside.

The actor Karel Roden played Rasputin.

RED SKULL (JOHANN SCHMIDT)

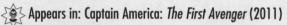 Appears in: Captain America: *The First Avenger* (2011)

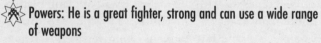 Powers: He is a great fighter, strong and can use a wide range of weapons

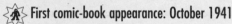 First comic-book appearance: October 1941

The Red Skull is Captain America's main opponent in *Captain America: The First Avenger*. He is the commander of HYDRA, a terrorist group. He is in charge of advanced weaponry for Hitler and wants to be the most powerful man in the world. In order to achieve this he needs the magical Tesseract (see quote below). His favourite weapon is a cigarette that fires his 'dust of death'. The red power is so poisonous that it kills the victim within seconds, leaving them with a red skull.

The actor chosen to play him was Hugo Weaving who is best known for playing Elrond in *The Lord of the Rings* and Agent Smith in *The Matrix* trilogy. He also provides the voice of Megatron in the *Transformers*' films.

Hugo talked to EW.com about his character. He said: 'Johann Schmidt is an ex-SS officer who has his own branch of the German Army under his command. He's a scientist who is interested in developing armaments and also developing and harnessing the power of a… of a… sort of unusual energy source which has spiritual connections [the Tesseract].'

RIDDLER (EDWARD NYGMA)

 Appears in: *Batman Forever* (1995)

Powers: Clever but not a fighter

First comic-book appearance: October 1948

The Riddler is one of two bad guys in the movie *Batman Forever*. The other bad guy is Two-Face.

Edward Nygma is an inventor who works for Wayne Enterprises. He comes up with the idea of a way of manipulating people's minds and takes his invention 'The Box' to Bruce Wayne. He expects praise but ends up being rejected – Bruce isn't a fan because it raises too many unanswerable questions.

After seeing Two-Face in a raid on TV, Edward decides that he needs a new name. He comes up with the name the Riddler and approaches Two-Face with a deal. He will tell him who Batman is if he helps The Box become a best seller. Two-Face agrees (after tossing a coin) and Edward gets his wish. Because 'The Box' allows Edward to read people's minds and steal their intelligence he becomes more and more intelligent as people rush out to buy their own boxes. No one guesses that Edward is the Riddler and he joins Two-Face on his crime sprees.

After the duo attack people at a party, they head to Wayne Manor because they know that Bruce is Batman. They wreck his equipment and kidnap his girlfriend Dr Chase Meridian, leaving him a riddle to solve. Batman and Robin solve it and rush to the Riddler's base together, only to get separated. Robin gets beaten by Two-Face and Batman is told by the Riddler that he has to choose who to save: will it be Chase or will it be Robin? Thankfully Batman doesn't have to choose and saves them both. He quickly destroys the brain-controlling system, which makes the Riddler suffer a mental breakdown.

The Riddler is admitted to Arkham Asylum and is so confused that he thinks he is Batman.

Lots of people wanted to play the Riddler, even Michael Jackson, but Jim Carrey was given the job. Jim had known the director for many years, before he was famous, and Joel Schumacher knew he would make a great Riddler. The studio rated him too because of his success as Ace Ventura Pet Detective in the film of the same name.

S IS FOR...

SABRETOOTH (VICTOR CREED)

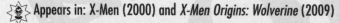 Appears in: X-Men (2000) and *X-Men Origins: Wolverine* (2009)

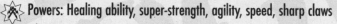 Powers: Healing ability, super-strength, agility, speed, sharp claws

First comic-book appearance: August 1977

Sabretooth is a mutant who belongs to Magneto's Brotherhood. He has tremendous strength, has super-senses, and can run on all fours thanks to his extendable claw-like fingernails. He tried to kidnap Rogue twice for Magneto but failed. He was blasted though the head by Cyclops's optic beams as the X-Men battled to save Rogue at the Statue of Liberty.

Sabretooth's past was explored in *X-Men Origins:Wolverine*. He is actually the half-brother of Wolverine whose real name is James Logan. They didn't realise they were brothers until James killed the man who murdered his father only to find out that he had been adopted and that the second man was his real father – meaning that Victor was his half-0brother. They ran away together and became soldiers fighting in various wars side by side. Victor tried to rape a woman in Vietnam, which led to them facing a firing squad, but the bullets just bounced off them. James remarks that they just tickled.

Major Stryker invites the brothers to join a special team of mutants he is putting together. Victor and James disagree over the methods of Team X – James isn't prepared to see innocent civilians slaughtered so he leaves the group. Victor won't leave and so the brothers separate for the first time.

Victor is very different to his kind-natured brother and will do anything for power. When Team X disbands he continues to work for Stryker, hunting down mutants so he can steal their abilities for his and Stryker's big plan. James has taken the name Logan and is trying to lead a normal life. They set him up to fall in love with Kayla Silverfox and then stage her death so it looks like Victor killed her. They know that they can get Logan to do what they want because seeing the love of his life dead destroys him and makes him open to Stryker's suggestion that he lets adamantium be fused with his skeleton. The metal is indestructible and turns Logan into the unstoppable Wolverine. As the procedure is taking place, Wolverine overhears Stryker mention to Agent Zero that his memory should be erased and quickly escapes. Stryker's superiors are furious because turning Wolverine into the ultimate weapon has cost half a billion dollars, and he's nowhere to be found.

Victor double-crossed his brother because Stryker promised to add adamantium to his skeleton too, but later retracted his offer because he said it would kill Victor. Although Wolverine hunts down Stryker and Victor, and fights his brother, the two end up working together to defeat Weapon XI. Victor won't let anyone else kill his brother and leaves once the battle ends.

Because Wolverine loses his memory after being shot in the head, he isn't aware that he is Sabretooth's brother once he joins Xavier and the X-Men.

The actor Liev Schreiber played Victor/Sabretooth in *X-Men Origins: Wolverine* and Tyler Mane played him in *X-Men*.

SANDMAN (FLINT MARKO)

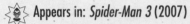 Appears in: *Spider-Man 3* (2007)

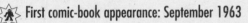 Powers: Ability to change his whole body into any shape made from sand

First comic-book appearance: September 1963

Flint Marko is a criminal who gains superhuman abilities when he falls into a particle accelerator as he's trying to escape from prison. The machine fuses his particles with the nearby sand, turning him into the Sandman.

Spider-Man learns from the police that the Sandman is the man who killed his Uncle Ben. The man they had thought was responsible, Dennis Carradine, was just Flint's accomplice and it had been Flint who fired the gun. Spider-Man feels bad because Dennis died after he chased him to a warehouse two years previously. Although he'd been a criminal he wasn't a murderer. He starts to picture Dennis trying to stop Flint on the night his uncle was killed. He decides that it is payback time!

Spider-Man, wearing his new black suit, tracks down the Sandman to an underground subway tunnel and they fight. Spider-Man thinks that he has killed him when he blasts him with water and the Sandman turns into mud. He hasn't, though, and later has to face him again when he teams up with Venom.

Venom and the Sandman kidnap Mary Jane and suspend her in a taxi above a building site. Spider-Man is back in his normal suit and calls on Harry to help him defeat the Sandman and Venom. After Venom is defeated Flint (Sandman) tells Peter what really happened the night his uncle was killed. Flint had been trying to steal his car and Uncle Ben had been trying to convince him not to when Dennis returned with the stolen money and touched his arm. This made him shoot the gun without thinking, killing Uncle Ben. Flint couldn't believe what had happened and refused to get in the car with Dennis, which meant that he didn't get caught. Flint had regretted his actions ever since and only did the robbery in the first place to try and help his terminally ill daughter who urgently needed expensive medical treatment to save her life. Peter decides to forgive Flint and Flint disappears.

The actor chosen to play the Sandman was Thomas Haden Church. Texan actor Thomas told FutureMovies.co.uk: 'Physically, I started training for the role about two years ago and I did about 97 per cent of my stunts, which for a guy in his forties is a pretty high percentage... I'm an older guy and I got injured in a variety of ways during filming but thankfully it was nothing lasting and nothing that was disabling while we were shooting. There was one sequence where I had to do something that was considered terrifically dangerous involving a lot of machinery and various cameras. The director only wanted me to do it once. I think that had something to do with insurance, but I convinced him to let me do it again – and it was extreme.

'But you know what? The CG [Computer Graphics] is so amazing now – Tobey and I aren't even in some of the fighting scenes. It's just my hair and his hair fighting – the rest is all CG! That's how it all works in the big time.'

SCANLON

Appears in: *The Green Hornet* (2011)

Powers: None but controls crime in Los Angeles alongside Bloodnofsky

First comic-book appearance: n/a

District Attorney Scanlon is one of the bad guys in *The Green Hornet*. He killed Britt's dad when he failed to do what he wanted and he attempts to do the same to Britt when he arranges for the Green Hornet to kill him (not realising that Britt is the Green Hornet). Scanlon thinks he can outsmart anyone and when the SWAT team arrive at the newspaper offices after the place has been destroyed by Scanlon, Bloodnofsky and their cronies, he tries to get them to arrest the Green Hornet instead. Britt isn't going to let him get away with murdering his dad and hits him with what remains of his car Black Beauty. Scanlon crashes through the window and falls ten floors down. Now he's dead he can no longer control Los Angeles crime world with Bloodnofsky.

The part of Scanlon was played by David Harbour.

SCARECROW (DR JONATHAN CRANE)

Appears in: *Batman Begins* (2005), *The Dark Knight* (2008)

Powers: Uses fear gas to drive his victims insane

First comic-book appearance: 1941

Dr Jonathan Crane works at Arkham Asylum. He is more than willing to certify that the men who work for mob boss Carmine

Falcone are mentally unfit for prison because Carmine is helping ship a poisonous toxin into Gotham for him. Crane is a cruel man who experiments on the patients at the asylum. When Carmine makes demands, Crane sprays him with the toxin, causing the once powerful man to break down and lose his mind. He wears a sack over his head, which acts as a gas mask so that he doesn't breathe in the toxin himself.

Crane's toxin makes victims hallucinate and see the thing they fear the most.

Crane attacks Batman with the gas but thankfully Alfred manages to save him with an anti-toxin. Rachel too is attacked when Crane lures her to the asylum to show her that the toxin is in Gotham's water network – and has been for several weeks. Batman gives Crane a taste of his own medicine by using his toxin against him. He then saves Rachel with the anti-toxin before heading out to stop Crane and Ra's al Ghul's plan from working. He won't let fear destroy Gotham City.

In *The Dark Knight* Crane is again masquerading as the Scarecrow and is trying to do a deal with some small-time gangsters in a car park before he gets interrupted by vigilantes pretending to be Batman. The gangsters are not happy with what Crane's 'drug' has done to their customers because they want them to keep coming back for more and not suffer mental breakdowns. The real Batman shows up and apprehends the Scarecrow. It's thought that he will be sent straight back to Arkham Asylum.

The actor Cillian Murphy played the Scarecrow.

DID YOU KNOW?

Cillian actually wanted to play the part of Batman but Christopher Nolan the director decided he'd make a much better Scarecrow.

SEBASTIAN SHAW

⚜ Appears in: *X2* (2003), *X-Men: First Class* (2011)

⚜ Powers: Ability to absorb kinetic energy and use it to become stronger than his opponents

⚜ First comic-book appearance: January 1980

Sebastian Shaw is a mutant who can take skills and other abilities from mutants and humans that he comes into contact with. He is a billionaire businessman and doesn't want people to know that he's a mutant, so keeps it well hidden. He isn't a nice guy and will do whatever it takes to get what he wants.

Sebastian had a minor cameo in the *X2* movie, disagreeing with Hank McCoy on TV. The actor who played him was Charles Siegel. Sebastian was given a much bigger role in *X-Men: First Class* where Golden Globe-winning actor Kevin Bacon was chosen to portray him.

Kevin revealed what sort of man/mutant he is to Moviefone: 'He's kind of a self-made man. He lost his father as a young man, made his first million by the time he was 30 and first billion by the time he was 40. He's a very powerful billionaire and also, as it turns out, a mutant. He's the leader of the Hellfire Club, which is a nightclub for the rich and extremely powerful. And he has a plot to take over the world, so that's really fun.

'He's incredibly good at manipulating people and at taking whatever kind of energy or ability they have and using it to his advantage, like if he's talking to a German, he's fluent in German. He's very charming and able to get whatever he wants.'

He revealed how playing Sebastian was difficult at times when he said: 'I have a really newfound appreciation for those actors, Heath Ledger, Johnny Depp, Robert Downey Jr, and Hugh Jackman, that are able to work within this kind of genre with all the green screen, and create great, memorable performances. It's very difficult; for me the most fun is always connecting on a scene and working with another actor to try to make that scene work. There was a scene near the end of the film between me and Michael Fassbender [Magneto] and the scene was okay, but I don't think either one of us was figuring it out. So Matthew let us spend a weekend up at his house and really figured it out from an acting standpoint, what this moment really means between these two.'

SILVER SURFER (NORRIN RADD)

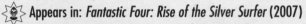

Appears in: *Fantastic Four: Rise of the Silver Surfer* (2007)

Powers: Travels faster than the speed of light, his board is his power source; the ability to channel cosmic energy and healing abilities

First comic-book appearance: March 1966

Because he leaves huge craters over places he visits, the Silver Surfer is seen initially as an evil destroyer of worlds by the Fantastic Four and the US government. Reed, one of the Fantastic Four, tracks where he has been and discovers that planets die after the Silver Surfer has paid them a visit. They later find out that he is a servant of Galactus, who is the real destroyer as he needs to feed off life supportingplanets. He sends the Silver Surfer ahead of him to find the planets.

The Silver Surfer gets his power from his board, a homing device that summons Galactus. He agreed to be his servant so that Galactus would spare his home planet, and the woman he loves.

In the film, the Silver Surfer unwittingly causes Reed and Sue to cancel their wedding and releases Victor von Doom as he flies past Latveria. The cosmic energy from the Silver Surfer turns Doom from a statue to a human being again. Doom has lost a lot of his power from being a statue for two years so tries to convince the Silver Surfer to join forces with him, but when he refuses and turns to go Doom blasts him in the back. The Silver Surfer quickly hits back, the power of his attack leaving Doom in an ice cave. Doom notices how his hand starts to heal and realises that the power from the blast is healing his whole body.

Being in contact with the Silver Surfer changes Johnny too, as he can now switch powers with other members of the Fantastic Four just by touching them. This helps them defeat Doom when he steals the Silver Surfer's board. The Fantastic Four had already taken the board from the Silver Surfer but Doom snuck in and stole it because he wanted the power it gives its rider.

The Silver Surfer is fond of Sue and ends up using his powers to bring her back to life after Doctor Doom stabs her shortly before he is defeated. She reminds the Silver Surfer of the girl he loves from his home planet and it is because of Sue and the kindness that she showed him that he decides to rebel against his boss Galactus.

He flies into the cloud-like Galactus, which causes them to be engulfed in a cosmic rift and destroys them both. Earth and the rest of the universe are safe once more.

After the credits, it was hinted that the Silver Surfer is not dead as he was shown floating in space, opening his eyes, and with his board heading towards him.

Doug Jones played the Silver Surfer but his suit was enhanced post-production. Laurence Fishburne provided his voice.

SINESTRO

 Appears in: *Green Lantern* (2011)

 Powers: Yellow ring, powered by fear, that allows him to create anything he wishes

 First comic-book appearance: August 1961

Sinestro is a Green Lantern and once Hal Jordan joins the Green Lantern Corps he sets about training him and becomes his mentor. Sinestro has red skin, a large forehead and a moustache which makes him look evil. Sinestro isn't Hal's biggest fan from the start because he isn't sure that a human has what it takes to become a Green Lantern. He is a strict teacher and starts off being a good guy, but this soon changes.

The actor who plays Sinestro is Mark Strong. Asked by Collider.com how he prepared himself for the role, he replied: 'I'm not sure you prepare for villains, necessarily. You prepare for a character. The way I look at villains is that nobody's born evil. Usually something happens to their time on the planet, or in space, that causes them to become that. You have to look at who the character is, what he stands for and what he believes in. He is an incredibly organised, fearless exponent of the Green Lantern corps, who believes he knows best. In this movie, as it stands, he becomes a mentor to the newly minted human Green Lantern, and guides him through his first steps. We deal with that process.

'I don't think of him as a villain. He's just an incredibly powerful presence who knows what he believes and what he wants to be right. If there's anything that causes him to spill over to the dark side later on, it's his unquestioning belief in his rightness.'

T IS FOR...

TOAD (MORTIMER TOYNBEE)

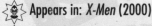 Appears in: *X-Men* (2000)

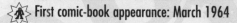 Powers: Superhuman legs and a flexible spine that allow him to leap and move like a toad; huge tongue that he uses as a weapon

First comic-book appearance: March 1964

Toad is a mutant who is a member of Magneto's Brotherhood. He has the abilities of a toad: he can leap, has a long sticky tongue which he uses as a weapon, and is very agile. His spit is very dangerous as it full of acid that hardens on impact and can stop his victims from breathing. He is one of the mutants who worked on Magneto's machine.

He was killed by Storm during the battle at the Empire State Building when she used her ability to create wind and lightning to electrocute him and he ended up in the Hudson River.

Toad was played by Ray Park in *X-Men*.

TWO-FACE (HARVEY DENT)

☠ Appears in: *Batman* (1989), *Batman Forever* (1995), *The Dark Knight* (2008)

☠ Powers: None but lacks morals and will kill a child; flips his two-headed coin to make decisions

☠ First comic-book appearance: August 1942

Harvey Dent is the District Attorney of Gotham and he is a man who won't be intimidated by the mob bosses that run crime in the city. He has only just been given the job and wants to make a big impression. He is the fiancé of Rachel Dawes, Bruce Wayne's first love.

Harvey carries a double-headed coin with him at all times, which he uses to tell him what to do in certain situations even though he already knows the outcome. It used to belong to his dad.

When the Joker wants to test Batman, he makes him decide whether to save Rachel Dawes or Harvey Dent from being blown to smithereens having placed them at opposite ends of the city with barrels of oil bombs set to detonate. Batman tells James Gordon and the police to go and rescue Harvey and he will rescue Rachel. Harvey tries to escape on hids own but only manages to knock his chair over and get spilt oil on half of his face.

When Batman gets to Rachel's address he finds Harvey. He saves Harvey, although his face is disfigured by the blast because of the oil he already had on his face. Rachel dies. Harvey had asked Batman to leave him and save Rachel instead but there hadn't been time. Harvey is devastated that the woman he loved died – as is Bruce because he loved Rachel, too.

While this is going on the Joker escapes the police station where he was being held and gives Batman another order. He wants Wayne Enterprises's accountant dead within an hour or he will blow up a hospital. Batman can't kill the man and the Joker visits his chosen hospital, speaks to a recovering Harvey, and then calmly walks out of the building wearing a nurse's uniform and uses his detonator to set off explosions.

Harvey becomes Two-Face; having burnt his face and lived through the explosion whilst Rachel died has made him lose his mind and he no longer wants to be a law-abiding citizen. He decides to take out his anger on Lieutenant James Gordon who failed to save Rachel in time. He is angry because the two corrupt cops who gave Rachel and himself to the Joker had been under investigation in the past but Gordon had trusted them. He kills the two cops and then decides that Gordon needs to learn first-hand what it's like to lose someone you love, and so kidnaps his family. He wants to kill whoever Gordon loves the most, and after pointing his gun at Gordon's wife's head he takes his son.

He then goes to flip his coin to see whether he should kill Gordon's son or let him live. Thankfully Batman arrives in time and tells Two-Face to leave the boy alone and judge the three men (Batman, Two-Face and Gordon) for giving the Joker so much control by making the mob gangs turn to him in the first place. Batman says the Joker chose to hurt Harvey because he was the best of them.

Two-Face flips the coin for Batman, and shoots him, then holds his gun and flips for himself. He doesn't shoot. Finally, when he's meant to be flipping the coin for Gordon, he changes his mind and flips for Gordon's son again, desperate to shoot him and make Gordon pay. As the coin is still in the air Batman manages to tackle him and he falls out of the building, taking

Gordon's son with him. Thankfully Batman manages to cling onto the boy and Gordon grabs him and lifts him to safety. Batman can't hold onto the beam and falls, hitting the ground. Gordon rushes down and is glad Batman hasn't been killed, but Two-Face is dead. They both see it as a tragedy because he was such a good man and the Joker has done what he set out to do. Everything good was built on Harvey's reputation. Batman can't bear to think of the Joker winning so tells Gordon he will take the rap for the murders Harvey committed. No one will know about the monster he became in the end.

Harvey/Two-Face was played by Aaron Eckhart in *The Dark Knight*. The characters also appeared in earlier Batman films. Billy Dee Williams played Harvey in *Batman* (1989) but it was only a small role. In *Batman Forever*, Two-Face was played by Tommy Lee Jones, who teamed up with the Riddler to kill Batman. In that movie Two-Face blamed Batman for failing to stop a mobster boss who threw acid in his face and turned him into Two-Face. He died after losing his balance over a pit and falling to his death.

U IS FOR...

U-FOES

 Appears in: *The Avengers: Earth's Mightiest Heroes* TV series

 Powers: Various

 First comic-book appearance: December 1980

The U-Foes are a group of four people with incredible powers that they gained from being exposed to cosmic radiation. Simon Utrecht, Mike Steel, Jimmy Darnell and Ann Darnell wanted to be like the Fantastic Four, they headed into space to recreate what happened to Reed, Sue, Johnny and Ben.

Simon became Vector who can fly and also repel and attract objects. Mike became Ironclad, and gained a metal-like skin and super-strength. Jimmy became X-Ray, a living energy field who can blast his enemies with radiation. He can also fly and make

94

himself invisible. Ann became Vapor, which allows her to become any gas she wishes. To defeat her enemies she becomes a poisonous gas and enters them.

Their worst enemy is Bruce Banner (the Hulk).

V IS FOR...

VENOM (EDDIE BROCK)

 Appears in: *Spider-Man 3* (2007)

 Powers: Shares the same powers as Spider-Man: super-strength, ability, speed and ability to project web string

 First comic-book appearance: March 1988

Eddie Brock is a freelance photographer who goes up against Peter Parker for the staff job. He wants to go out with Gwen Stacy, but she just wants to be friends. Eddie takes some photos of her to help her become a model and gets really angry when Peter goes on a date with her. He wants the *Daily Bugle* job so much that he fakes some shots of Spider-Man robbing a bank. Peter tells the editor they are fakes and Eddie gets the sack.

Eddie is really upset and angry, and instead of blaming himself for ruining his chances of getting the job he blames Peter. He goes to a church and prays that God will kill Peter.

Peter also heads to the church, desperate to remove his black suit, which is destroying him. He goes to the top of the church tower and tries to rip the suit from his face but the symbiote just won't let go. He knocks against the church bell and notices how the symbiote hates the noise. He rings the bell and screams out in pain, as the process of removing the suit is very painful. Eddie recognises Peter's voice and goes to the bottom of the stairs that lead to the top of the tower. He watches as the symbiote peels off Peter and falls from the church tower, and lands on him. It takes over his body, bringing him to his knees and turning him into Venom.

Eddie has more control over the symbiote than Peter did and it starts exaggerating his worse character traits straightaway. He wanted Peter to die when he was merely Eddie and so now he's Venom he wants him dead even more. He joins up with the Sandman and together they kidnap Mary Jane and dangle her in a taxi over a building site using Venom's web strings.

Peter enlists the help of Harry and together they take on the Sandman and Venom.

Harry ends up sacrificing himself when Venom tries to kill Spider-Man with Harry's glider. The glider stabs him in the chest, just like the glider did to his dad during his fight with Spider-Man. Spider-Man then uses the symbiote's hatred of loud noises to separate it from Eddie by using several pipes to pen Venom in and hitting them so they emit a loud noise. Spider-Man throws one of Harry's bombs at the symbiote to destroy it and grabs Eddie, but he wants the power the symbiote gives him so much that he tries to get it to reattach to him and stop the bomb going off. He ends up getting blown to pieces along with the symbiote. His greed and lust for power has destroyed him. Thank goodness Peter took off his black suit when he did otherwise he could have been destroyed by the symbiote instead!

The actor chosen to play Eddie and Venom was Topher Grace. He is most famous for playing Eric Forman in *That '70s Show*. Topher talked to journalist Martyn Palmer about what it was like to play Venom. He said: 'The suit is hot and it's pretty claustrophobic in there. And there's no zipper so you can't go to the bathroom! So that's the most challenging thing about being a supervillain. The days were long and challenging and sometimes, if I was playing Venom that day, uncomfortable. But then I would watch the playback later and say: "You know, that's the coolest shot I've probably ever seen..." So it was all about the destination and not the journey.'

He talked about the physical changes, too: 'I've never really worked out in my life and I had to put on 20 pounds, which still didn't look like a lot because I'm a very skinny guy. But it was about nine months of working out and eating in a different way. I knew that would be part of the process. There's a lot of physical stuff when you are working – there's a lot of hanging from wires and jumping around.'

W IS FOR...

WILLIAM STRYKER

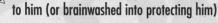 Appears in: *X2* (2003), *X-Men Origins: Wolverine* (2009)

 Powers: None but surrounds himself with mutants who are loyal to him (or brainwashed into protecting him)

 First comic-book appearance: 1982

William Stryker is a human. He loves mutants but despises them deeply too, because his son, who is a mutant, caused his wife to commit suicide by putting thoughts into her head. He likes using mutants for his own gains and experimenting on them, but he doesn't feel that they matter at all. He will wipe their memories and kill them if he needs to.

Stryker is a Major in the army when he approaches Logan and Victor in their prison cell to ask them to join him and his team of mutants. He is impressed that they survived being shot at by a firing squad without gaining even a scratch. They agree to join Team X and at first it looks like they have found somewhere they belong until Logan finds out that Stryker doesn't care if innocent humans are killed during their missions. Stryker might be lacking in morals but Logan isn't and decides to walk away. His brother Victor refuses and becomes Stryker's number two.

Victor does what Stryker tells him and many years after Team X is disbanded he's sent out to kill all the mutants who were in the team, and steal their powers so that Stryker can use them in his master plan. He fakes Kayla's (Logan's girlfriend's) death so that Logan will be more open to Stryker's suggestion that he join his programme, and allow adamantium to be fused with his skeleton to make him indestructible. Stryker wants to use Wolverine (Logan) as a weapon, but his plans are ruined when Wolverine overhears Stryker mention to Agent Zero that his memory should be erased and quickly escapes. Stryker's superiors are furious as to turn Wolverine into the ultimate weapon cost half a billion dollars. Stryker uses Wade Wilson to make Weapon XI (Deadpool), a mutant with the abilities of many. Stryker murders General Munson when he tries to stop his experiments and Weapon XI.

Stryker always promised that he would add adamantium to Victor's skeleton too, but later retracted his offer because he says it would kill Victor. Stryker is not a man of his word and can't be trusted.

Although Wolverine hunts down Stryker and Victor, and fights his brother, they end up joining together to defeat Weapon XI. Stryker shoots Wolverine in the head with bullets made from adamantium as he helps the young mutants escape. Kayla manages to controls Stryker's mind and tells him to drop the gun and keep walking, even when his feet bleed. She then dies but Wolverine survives as his body heals itself, although his memory has been damaged because of the bullets. He doesn't recognise Kayla when he sees her dead body.

Stryker eventually gets caught by the military police as he is walking along and they question him about the murder of General Munson.

Stryker appears in the *X2* movie too, and 20 years have passed. He is still a scientist interested in weapons. It is explained that he sent his mutant son Jason to Xavier's school to be cured, only to discover that Xavier teaches mutants to embrace their abilities and not to get rid of them. Jason becomes a troubled young man and starts to hate the people/mutants around him. After he caused his mother to commit suicide, Stryker decides to cut out part of Jason's brain to try and alter his behaviour and make him easier to control.

Stryker uses his son's powers to control and see inside other peoples' brains. Stryker and Jason brainwash Magneto, Cyclops and Xavier. Earlier he had used fluid from Jason to brainwash Nightcrawler into trying to kill the President of the United States. He has Xavier change the Cerebro II to kill mutants, only for Magneto to instruct Mystique to take on the body shape of Stryker and trick Jason into making Xavier change the machine so that it kills humans not mutants.

Xavier is powerless until Storm and Nightcrawler manage to disrupt the messages that Jason is sending to Xavier's brain. He can then stop the machine. Stryker ends up dying after both Wolverine and Magneto refuse to let him escape. Magneto ties Stryker to some debris so he can't leave and after Stryker asks Wolverine some questions about his past he leaves him to die. Wolverine doesn't kill him but he doesn't save him either.

Stryker was played by Brian Cox in *X2* and Danny Huston played him in *X-Men Origins: Wolverine*. Danny played Poseidon in *Clash of the Titans* and Richard the Lionheart in *Robin Hood*. Brian is best known for his role in the 1986 film *Manhunter*.

 **IS FOR...**

XANDU

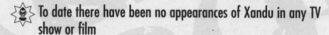 To date there have been no appearances of Xandu in any TV show or film

Powers: Sorcery, hypnotism

First comic-book appearance: 1965

Xandu is a sorcerer who has half the Wand of Watoomb. The wand gives its owner great power: the ability to heal injuries, create force fields, open portals to other dimensions... and Xandu must have it.

The other half of the wand belongs to Doctor Strange and taking it isn't going to be easy. He sends out a robot army but they are no match for Doctor Strange and Spider-Man. They easily defeat them and Xandu must think of another way to get his hands on the second half. He needs it so he can save his wife who is currently in a coma.

Y IS FOR...

YURIKO OYAMA (LADY DEATHSTRIKE)

 Appears in: *X2* (2003)

 Powers: Similar to Wolverine: super-strength, ability to heal, virtually unstoppable, five metal claws on each hand

 First comic-book appearance: August 1983

Yuriko Oyama is a mutant who was experimented on by William Stryker and, like Wolverine, ended up having adamantium added to her spine. But Stryker made sure that he brainwashed her so she couldn't escape like Wolverine did. She is a trained assassin and was sent to capture Cyclops and Xavier when they went to visit Magneto in his plastic cell.

She has claws like Wolverine but Stryker gave her five claws on each hand rather than three. She fights Wolverine when he tries to follow Stryker out of the lab where they were both 'created' and shows immense strength and agility. Both Wolverine and Yuriko have the healing ability so they are each impossible to kill in the traditional way. They stab each other with their claws and it looks like their battle could go on forever until Wolverine injects her with liquid adamantium. The metal fluid seeps out of her mouth, her nose and her eyes. Wolverine didn't want to kill her but he had no choice.

The actress chosen to play Yuriko was Kelly Hu.

Z IS FOR...

ZOOM (HUNTER ZOLOMON)

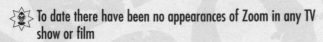

⚡ To date there have been no appearances of Zoom in any TV show or film

⚡ Powers: Can control time, super-speed

⚡ First comic-book appearance: November 2001

Hunter Zolomon had a horrible start in life. His father murdered six girls and then his own wife when she reported him to the police – and was then shot by the police. Hunter had never got on with his parents but he had no idea what his father was doing.

He became an expert in psychology and criminology at college and then joined the FBI. He married his girlfriend Ashley and things were going well until he misjudged a criminal called the Clown and ended up getting shot in the kneecap. Ashley's dad also died during the gunfire. Both Ashley and the FBI blamed Hunter and he soon found himself divorced and jobless.

Finding his next job was tricky because the once-active Hunter had been reduced to using a cane and struggled to walk. He ended up working as a profiler in the Police Department of Metahuman Hostilities. He met Flash and they became good friends, although Hunter always wished he could be the one catching the bad guys.

He was attacked by the villain Gorilla Grodd, and ended up paralysed after he broke his back. He asked Flash if he could use his cosmic treadmill to go back in time and stop it happening, but Flash refused. Hunter was so desperate he went behind Flash's back and tried to use it, but it caused a huge explosion which changed his connection to time. This gave him the ability to change the speed he moves in time, meaning that he could run even faster than Flash.

Hunter decided to call himself Zoom and help Flash become a better superhero. To do this he felt that Flash needed a personal tragedy as he had never had anything really bad happen to him. Zoom decided that the best way to do this would be to kill his pregnant wife Linda. Flash managed to stop him killing her but his wife miscarried and lost the twins she was carrying.

SUPERHEROES V SUPERVILLAINS A-Z

SARAH OLIVER

JB
JOHN BLAKE

Published by John Blake Publishing Ltd,
3 Bramber Court, 2 Bramber Road,
London W14 9PB, England

www.johnblakepublishing.co.uk

www.facebook.com/Johnblakepub facebook
twitter.com/johnblakepub twitter

First published in paperback in 2011

ISBN: 978 1 84358 420 9

British Library Cataloguing-in-Publication Data:

A catalogue record for this book is available from the British Library.

Design by www.envydesign.co.uk

Printed and bound by CPI Group (UK) Ltd, Croydon, CR0 4YY

3 5 7 9 10 8 6 4 2

Papers used by John Blake Publishing are natural, recyclable products made
from wood grown in sustainable forests. The manufacturing processes conform
to the environmental regulations of the country of origin.

Every attempt has been made to contact the relevant copyright-holders,
but some were unobtainable. We would be grateful if the appropriate
people could contact us.

ABOUT THE AUTHOR

Sarah Oliver is a journalist who loves Superhero movies. Her favourite three Superheroes of all time are Superman, Wolverine and the Hulk. This book is dedicated to her husband Jon who helped with the writing and editing of this book. His favourite three Superheroes are Spider-Man, Batman and Iron Man.

OTHER A–Z BOOKS BY SARAH OLIVER

SUPERHEROES A-Z

THE ULTIMATE GUIDE TO THE GREATEST SUPERHEROES OF ALL TIME

This book is jam-packed with the biggest and best Superheroes there have ever been. We've carefully selected over 60 of your favourite Superheroes to be in this *Superheroes A–Z*!

It includes all your DC favourites like Batman and Superman, and all your favourite Marvel heroes like Iron Man and Spider-Man. There are plenty of new Superheroes that you might never have heard of before but who will be appearing in the new Superhero movies that are coming to cinemas soon!

If you want to learn about the new X-Men mutants or find out more about the Green Arrow Corps, then you'll find it all inside. You'll discover all the behind-the-scenes secrets, including how they made sure that Ben Affleck couldn't see during *Daredevil*, why Samuel L. Jackson was disappointed the first time he saw *Iron Man* and what happened when the Batmobile was being driven to the set.

You can read this book from start to finish, or dip in and out of it, as you prefer. Once you've read all about the greatest Superheroes of all time, flip the book over and learn all about their enemies in *Supervillains A–Z*.

A IS FOR...

ABE SAPIEN

Appears in: *Hellboy* (2004) and *Hellboy II: The Golden Army* (2008)

Powers: Can survive under water for long periods of time; telepathy

First comic-book appearance: 1994

Abe Sapien is a merman–type creature who has psychic powers. He works for the B.P.R.D. (Bureau for Paranormal Research and Defence), which is a secret US Government Agency, alongside Hellboy. The agency's mission is to protect the USA from the paranormal, supernatural and the occult. He has a strange appearance, with a head shaped rather like a dolphin and a body almost like a man. Abe goes by the nickname 'Blue' and Hellboy goes by the nickname 'Red'. He needs to be in water to survive but can walk around normally if wearing a

special helmet that supplies water to his gills. He doesn't eat normal food and instead prefers to munch on eggs that are thousands of years old. He spends a lot of his time in his aquarium in Professor Bruttenholm's office.

The actor who plays Abe in the *Hellboy* movies is Doug Jones but his voice was not used for the first film. Instead *Frasier* actor David Hyde Pierce's voice was chosen. David felt that Doug alone deserved to be known as Abe, so he refused to be credited. He didn't take part in any press interviews and didn't even turn up to the premiere. Doug was very grateful for the kindness David showed him although they had never even met. He was even happier when he found out that he was being allowed to provide Abe's voice in the second *Hellboy* film. The part was 100 per cent his own!

Abe wasn't the only character that Doug played in the *Hellboy* movies. He also played the Angel of Death and Chamberlain.

DID YOU KNOW?

Doug played the Silver Surfer in the second *Fantastic Four* movie, but as with the first *Hellboy* film, his voice wasn't used, just his body.

He talked about how frustrating it was to Devin Faraci from Chud.com. Doug said: 'Everybody loved the voice that I had affected for the Surfer. In the end, 20th Century Fox is really good at marketing films and part of getting butts in seats are celebrity names. I'm not really sure that the 20th Century Fox people understood the ever-powerful geek fan base that follows me. I'm not sure that they were aware of that even, but Laurence Fishburne has some geek fan base and some mainstream, and so he pulled it all in and that's fine. I understand that part and whatever business had to take place, but artistically from my standpoint it was disappointing to lose my voice in that way.'

ANGEL (WARREN WORTHINGTON III)

✨ Appears in: *X-Men: The Last Stand* (2006), *X-Men: First Class* (2011)

✨ Powers: Ability to fly; enhanced senses, endurance, speed and reflexes

✨ First comic-book appearance: September 1963

Warren is the son of a rich industrialist who seeks to develop a cure for mutants. Warren first discovered that he was a mutant when he was a young boy and tried to cut off the stumps that would become his wings. He is a prisoner and he is going to become the first mutant to receive the cure, until he decides that being a mutant might not be that bad after all. He breaks his chains and knocks over those trying to administer the drugs to cure him. He talks to his father before leaping through the window and flying to Xavier's School for the Gifted.

Later, Angel is forced to rescue his father who is thrown from a roof by an enraged Arclight, Quill and Psylocke during the final showdown.

Two actors were chosen to play Angel in *X-Men: The Last Stand*. Ben Foster played the older Angel and Cayden Boyd played the younger James in the flashback.

Ben was thrilled to be chosen to play Angel and told TheCinemaSource.com what it was like to be on the X-Men set: 'Coming to work, it's like coming to work in an amusement park. We get to get tied to wires and dropped out of things, except they pay you do it. It's a good gig.'

He didn't actually get to fly because those parts of the film were computer generated, but for the scenes where he is walking about he had giant wings strapped to his back.

ANGEL SALVADORE

⚙ Appears in: *X-Men: First Class* (2011)

☠ Powers: Ability to fly, can create an ultrasonic sound

✦ First comic-book appearance: 2001

Angel is a mutant who doesn't have an alias. She just uses her real name. Her abilities are similar to those of a housefly: she has wings that she can use to fly and to create an ultrasonic sound that deafens her enemies. She also lays eggs and can produce an acid-like liquid from her mouth which allows her to digest her food.

In the comics, she didn't have a good childhood thanks to her step-father, and left home when she was 14. She lived in the woods and was captured by a group of humans called the U-Men. The U-Men didn't care about mutants and killed them for their mutant parts. They admired Angel's wings and wanted them for themselves. Thankfully she was rescued just in time.

The actress chosen to play Angel was Zoë Kravitz. We will have to wait and see how Angel is portrayed in *X-Men: First Class* and whether her backstory is the same as it is in the comics.

AVENGERS

⚙ Appear in: *The Avengers* (2012), and various movies as individuals

☠ Powers: Various

✦ First comic-book appearance: September 1963

The Avengers are a team of superheroes who have to work together to defeat their enemies, who are too powerful to be

defeated by one superhero working alone. In *The Avengers* film, the members of the Avengers that will be focused on are: Iron Man, Thor, Black Widow, Hawkeye, Captain America, War Machine and Hulk. In the comics there have been a lot more members over the years. The most important ones have been Iron Man, Thor, Wasp, Hulk, Ant-Man I and II, Wonderman, Captain America, Hawkeye, Scarlet Witch, Vision, Quicksilver, Black Widow, Black Panther, Hercules, She-Hulk, Black Knight, Pulsar, Crystal and Quasar.

The group was originally formed a short time after the Fantastic Four started working as a superhero team. Members join and leave all the time, depending on the situation in hand. Their base is the Avengers Mansion, which used to belong to Tony Stark. Over the years they have faced some horrible supervillains, the worst being, Kang, Space Phantom, the Mole Men, the Lava Men, Baron Zemo, Electro, Madame Hydra, Sauron, Grandmaster and Collector. Occasionally they call on the Fantastic Four to help them.

The Avengers movie is due to be released on 4 May 2012. Studio bosses at Marvel have been planning since 2005 to bring out the film but wanted to release films about the individual members first.

It was not known when the film was first discussed whether Captain America or Iron Man would be leading the team. Chris Evans told MTV after he was cast as Captain America: 'I don't know if they're going to make him [Captain America] the boss... I don't think anybody tells Downey [Robert Jr] what to do, and that's what makes [him] Downey.'

All the cast felt under pressure to make sure *The Avengers* movie was the best it could be. They didn't want fans of the comics to be disappointed.

AQUAMAN

 Appears in: Various cartoon series

Powers: Telepathy, magical hand, ability to communicate with sea life, breathe underwater and swim 3,000 metres in a second

First comic-book appearance: November 1941

Aquaman is King of the Seven Seas. His mother was Queen Atlanna and his father was Atlan. His people sentenced him to death once he started communicating with animals because they believed it was a sign of the monster Kordax. Before he could die on Mercy Reef he was found by a dolphin called Porm, who looked after him until lighthouse keeper Arthur Curry rescued him. He learned a lot from the man, who became his adoptive father and even started to call himself Arthur Curry.

Years later, he witnessed a fight between Flash and the Frankster. The Flash encouraged him to go with him the USA, which he did, and became one of the first members of the Justice League of America. He returned to his kingdom a superhero and became the King of Atlantis.

In November 2010 it was revealed that an Aquaman film is being planned but it won't be released until 2015 or 2016 because Warner Bros want to bring out the Flash and Wonderwoman movies first.

B IS FOR...

BANSHEE (SEAN CASSIDY)

- Appears in: *X-Men: First Class* (2011)
- Powers: Sonic scream
- First comic-book appearance: January 1967

Banshee is a mutant from Ireland with the ability to emit a 'sonic scream'. His scream can thrust him into the air, cause the things around him to shatter, as well as affecting the mutants around him. His scream can knock them out cold.

He was played in the film by virtual unknown Caleb Landry Jones, an actor from Texas. Caleb is a talented songwriter and musician too, but not many people have heard his music.

BATGIRL (BARBARA WILSON)

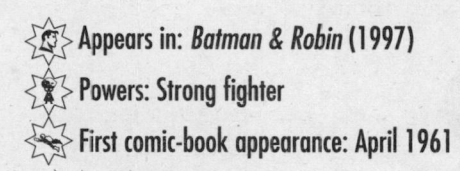

- Appears in: *Batman & Robin* (1997)
- Powers: Strong fighter
- First comic-book appearance: April 1961

Barbara Wilson is Alfred Pennyworth's niece, and after learning that he is ill she travels to Gotham to see him. She has been attending an English boarding school for many years after her parents were killed in a car crash. She is very close to him and wants to help him leave his butler days behind. She is devastated to learn that he has MacGregor's Syndrome and that there is no cure.

Bruce invites her to stay at Wayne Manor and she soon discovers his secret identity. Alfred hands her an encrypted disc containing all of Batman's secrets and she manages to hack into it. She wants to help and turns herself into Batgirl, wearing a suit that Alfred had specially made for her. It's a good job Alfred thought of his niece becoming a female superhero because it isn't long before Batman and Robin are in trouble. They have to defeat Mr Freeze, Poison Ivy and Bane, so need Batgirl to help them. Batgirl and Robin team up to defeat Bane, and Batgirl defeats Ivy single-handedly.

After Mr Freeze is defeated he hands over a cure for MacGregor's Syndrome, which ultimately saves Alfred's life. Barbara is over the moon that her uncle will no longer die.

The actress Alicia Silverstone played Barbara/Batgirl. In the film, Barbara has a crush on Dick Grayson/Robin, and this may have been developed had the next movie *Batman Triumphant* not been cancelled. *Batman & Robin* did not do as well as expected and critics hated it. They didn't like Mr Freeze's one-liners, the overall child-friendly approach and the acting of the main actors.

Alicia ended up getting the Razzie award for Worst Supporting Actress, which must have been very disappointing for her. She did win a Kids' Choice Award, though, because kids loved the film even if adults didn't!

She found the whole experience of being in a Batman movie really fun and told interviewers it was like being at a big party. After filming finished she wanted to slow down, catch up on sleep and spend time with her dogs.

BATMAN (BRUCE WAYNE)

Appears in: *Batman: The Movie* (1966), *Batman* (1989), *Batman Returns* (1992), *Batman Forever* (1995), *Batman & Robin* (1997), *Catwoman* (2004), *Batman Begins* (2005), *The Dark Knight* (2008), *The Dark Knight Rises* (2012)

Powers: Trained in all the different martial arts; high-tech body armour, gadgets, weapons and vehicles

First comic-book appearance: May 1939

Batman is one of the most loved superheroes of all time. He is the protector of Gotham City and fights for justice. The character of Batman first appeared in a comic book back in 1939 and since then there have been many more comic–book appearances, TV series, radio dramas and films on the caped crusader.

The first Batman movie came out in 1966 and saw Batman and Robin taking on the Joker, the Riddler, Penguin and Catwoman. Adam West played Batman in this film. The next one didn't come out for another 23 years. *Batman* was directed by Tim Burton and saw Michael Keaton play the lead role. There was no Robin this time around and his enemy was the Joker.

This film was a huge success and even won an Oscar!

Michael Keaton wasn't an obvious choice to play Batman

but he showed those who had objected to his being cast that they were wrong. He made a great Batman. He found wearing Batman's suit difficult because he doesn't like being in enclosed spaces and the suit was very tight and overpowering. Being stuck in the suit for hours at a time did help him get into character.

Michael also played Batman in the next film, *Batman Returns*, but decided not to play him for a third time because he didn't think the script for *Batman Forever* was strong enough. In the second Tim Burton/Michael Keaton movie Batman has to face Catwoman and Penguin. He was originally going to be joined by Robin but the decision was made to drop Robin from the cast because it was felt there were too many characters.

Batman Forever saw Val Kilmer play Batman/Bruce Wayne. In this film, Robin finally made an appearance and the villains were Two-Face and the Riddler. It is thought that Val Kilmer agreed to play Batman without having read a script. He did really well to secure the part because lots of other big names wanted to play Batman – Johnny Depp, Daniel Day-Lewis and Ralph Fiennes were considered before Val Kilmer got the big thumbs-up.

The director for this movie was Joel Schumacher and he didn't enjoying working with Val Kilmer. He found the actor difficult and didn't like the way he treated some members of the crew.

A different Batman was found for the next movie, *Batman & Robin*. George Clooney took on the role and had to defeat Mr Freeze, Poison Ivy and Bane… with the help of Robin and Batgirl. George filmed the movie alongside his *ER* commitments. He was able to film the hospital drama and the movie at the same time because they were filmed at the same studio lot. This movie wasn't a hit and the planned follow-up *Batman Triumphant* was never filmed.

The next Batman film saw a move back to the origins of Batman. The focus was no longer on the rivals that Batman

would be facing but on the man himself. The scriptwriters and producers wanted people to understand who Bruce Wayne and Batman really were. Christopher Nolan was brought on board to direct *Batman Begins*, and Christian Bale was cast as the leading man.

Christian Bale was seen as the perfect actor to play Batman and Bruce Wayne because he could play both characters equally well. Michael Keaton had been best at playing Bruce, whereas Val Kilmer's strength had been playing Batman – Christian was the first actor to excel in both roles.

In the film, it is revealed how Bruce fell down a well, witnessed his parents' murder, was imprisoned in Bhutan and is after revenge. He wants the people behind his parents' murder to pay for what they have done. After travelling the world he returns to Gotham, joins forces with Sergeant Jim Gordon and becomes Batman. He wants to clean up the city. In this movie Batman's enemies are Carmine Falcone, Ra's al Ghul and Scarecrow. The young Bruce in the flashback scenes was played by child actor Gus Lewis.

To prepare for the film Christian had to firstly gain around seven stone because he had lost a lot of weight since being cast. He had been playing an emaciated man in *The Machinist* and had been starving himself for months, so he looked like a skeleton. Producers on that movie had been so concerned by his weight loss that they had banned him from losing any more weight. Once *The Machinist* wrapped he started eating properly and working out with a personal trainer. He actually put on too much weight in the end, and looked too strong to play Bruce Wayne, so he had to lose a bit of weight before the people behind *Batman Begins* were happy.

Christian talked to journalist Rebecca Murray about the differences between *Batman Begins* and the earlier films. 'We were focusing on Bruce Wayne and Batman, whereas in watching most of the other movies, and also the TV series and things, I

always found the villains much more interesting,' he said. 'And that was the main revelation to me in reading one of the graphic novels. Batman is the most interesting of them all, you know? I mean, he's the really on-the-edge one because he's the guy that, okay, he's doing good, but he's the Dark Knight. I mean, a knight is meant to be in shining armour and he's the Dark Knight. He could do good things but man, he could just as easily flip over and become like the ultimate villain. Hopefully we've been able to portray that in a more character-based way than has been shown before.'

DID YOU KNOW?

A drunken man accidentally crashed into the Batmobile as it was being driven from one set to the next. Luckily no one was hurt, but according to Christian Bale the man's excuse was that he panicked when he saw the car and thought it was from outer space!

About.com asked Christian during an interview which of his predecessors had added the most credibility to the role of Batman. He replied: 'You know, they did it in different ways. I think what Adam West did was great. I just didn't realise when I was watching it as a kid that it was a spoof, you know? It was a very campy kind of thing, performance, that he was doing. After that, I would say Michael Keaton because of Tim Burton and the way that he approached the movie. However, we didn't want to do anything like that either. To me, that isn't what I was seeing in the graphic novels at all. And I'd never really felt the danger of Batman that I felt should be appropriate.

'It was also in reading a foreward by Frank Miller that I believe is in "Batman Year One" about when he first saw Batman and how he says to him Batman was never funny. And I liked that because that's what I had always thought. That this should

not be, that there can be a lot of comedy, but coming from other people. But the actual Batman himself, you know, I think had gotten lost in a lot of little one-liners and quips that reduced the edge and the reason that he had become this Batman in the first place, which was this incredible pain, anger, guilt and rage that he had within.'

Batman Begins was a massive success but the next Batman film was even bigger. *The Dark Knight* became one of the highest-grossing movies of all time. In this movie Christian Bale continued to play Batman, only this time his enemies were the Joker, played by Heath Ledger, and Two-Face, played by Aaron Eckhart. The director Christopher Nolan started planning the next movie in 2008 and filming for *The Dark Knight Rises* began in January 2011.

Before filming started Christopher Nolan confessed to the *Los Angeles Times*: 'Without getting into specifics, the key thing that makes the third film a great possibility for us is that we want to finish our story. And in viewing it as the finishing of a story rather than infinitely blowing up the balloon and expanding the story…' he said.

He went on: 'I'm very excited about the end of the film, the conclusion, and what we've done with the characters. My brother [*Dark Knight* co-writer Jonathan Nolan] has come up with some pretty exciting stuff. Unlike the comics, these things don't go on forever in film, and viewing it as a story with an end is useful. Viewing it as an ending, that sets you very much on the right track about the appropriate conclusion and the essence of what tale we're telling. And it harks back to that priority of trying to find the reality in these fantastic stories.'

BEAST (DR HENRY 'HANK' MCCOY)

Appears in: *X2* (2003), X-Men: *The Last Stand* (2006),
X Men: First Class (2011)

Powers: Highly intelligent, extremely strong, heightened senses,
night vision

First comic-book appearance: September 1963

The Beast was set to appear in the first *X-Men* film but the
character was cut because of problems with make-up. The
second movie, *X2*, was also going to include Beast in a
prominent role, but in the end he was missed out. Only his Dr
Hank McCoy side was shown, briefly, on a TV screen during
one scene. The actor who played Dr Hank McCoy was Steve
Bacic, but he was replaced by Kelsey Grammer in *X-Men: The
Last Stand*.

In the third *X-Men* movie we finally get to meet the Beast!
He is a huge blue-skinned mutant covered in fur. He has
superhuman strength and agility, and can easily beat most
opponents. He was one of the first X-Men and has long since
graduated from the Xavier Institute for Higher Learning. He
chose to get into politics and became the Secretary of Mutant
Affairs. He is also an excellent scientist and very intelligent.

The Beast doesn't oppose the mutant cure drug to start with
but once he finds out that it's being developed as a weapon he
isn't happy. He no longer wants to be the Secretary of Mutant
Affairs and resigns. He joins the X-Men and fights Magneto's
army – releasing his anger on them. He manages to inject
Magneto with the cure, which strips him of all his powers. Later,
the President makes him ambassador to the United Nations.

Kelsey found wearing the make-up required to play the Beast
very useful when it came to him getting into character. He

explained to The Cinema Source: 'You become enveloped by this material that feels like a second skin of sorts... you spend the rest of your day locked inside this character. It's a powerful tool for creating a memorable character that isn't one you've done before. It's an advantageous position to be in.

'If it's good make-up, it will influence your body language, it will affect the way you move. You take on physical manifestations of a look that's different; it's just an interesting part of what we do. Beast is cool looking, he's blue, he's got great hair, I haven't had great hair since I was 16! It's playing dress up!'

In *X-Men: First Class* the role of Beast went to *Skins* actor Nicholas Hoult. It was to be his biggest role yet, having previously acted alongside Hugh Grant in *About a Boy* and Sam Worthington in *Clash of the Titans*.

BLACK WIDOW (NATASHA ROMANOFF)

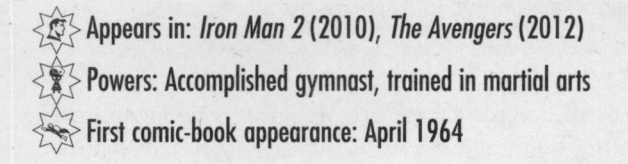

Appears in: *Iron Man 2* (2010), *The Avengers* (2012)

Powers: Accomplished gymnast, trained in martial arts

First comic-book appearance: April 1964

Actress Scarlett Johansson plays Black Widow in both *Iron Man 2* and *The Avengers*. It is thought that she will be given her own spin-off movie in the next two years.

In *Iron Man 2* Natasha Romanoff is pretending to be Natalie Rushman, Tony Stark's new assistant. She gets the job after Tony promotes Pepper Potts to CEO of Stark Industries. Tony likes her straight away, making Pepper a bit jealous as she is used to getting his attention. Natalie's real identity is revealed to Tony later when Nick Fury explains that she is undercover

S.H.I.E.L.D. spy Natasha Romanoff and her mission is to keep an eye on him!

Natasha/Black Widow has to help Happy Hogan (Tony's bodyguard and close friend) break into Hammer Industries and help Rhodey regain control of the Mark II armour so he can become War Machine and help Iron Man/Tony defeat the drones and Vanko.

Scarlett Johansson had been considered for other female superheroes in the Marvel universe before it was decided she would play Black Widow. She had met with *Iron Man* director Jon Favreau and producer Kevin Feige a few times before they decided she would be playing Black Widow in *Iron Man 2*. Up until that point they hadn't been sure whether to include the character in the film at all.

DID YOU KNOW?

For her second meeting with Jon, Scarlett decided to dye her hair red. Black Widow has red hair in the comics and she wanted to show Jon that she was willing to 'experiment' with her hair.

Scarlett was thrilled to get the opportunity to be in *Iron Man 2* and work alongside Robert Downey Jr and Gwyneth Paltrow. She told Rebecca Murray from About.com: 'I was such a fan of the first one… I was kind of geeked out by the movie to begin with. I think 80 per cent of the crew came back for the second time. I was really surprised to find that this movie that was kind of seemingly larger than life had such a small, sort of familial feeling on set. Even though we were making this huge movie, we had Kevin Feige there everyday. I don't know, it just felt like the whole studio was behind the movie in a really kind of supportive and nurturing way.'

Playing a classic superhero like Black Widow involves lots of

research, something Scarlett discovered. She knew who Black Widow was, she'd read the script but she needed to know her backstory. Scarlett explained: 'I was familiar with the character as far as I had researched different super-heroines. But I didn't know that much about the characters, background. Only that she was kind of the oldest of the super heroines and has this incredible fan base. She's had many incarnations. I think that the research I did was mostly a lot of the stunt work that I put into it. The character herself I think remains quite mysterious, which is important. She's covert.'

She explained that she thought the character was some sort shape-shifter: 'It was sort of like playing two different characters. One character that is more kind of mysterious, I don't want to say submissive, but she's blending in with the crowd, I suppose. The other part of this character is someone who is assertive and knows their sh*t. She's able to just say, "I'm going to fight this head on." For me, being able to have that kind of feeling, being able to be competent enough to sell it, that this is somebody who is going to kick some ass and don't for a second doubt that she's going to follow through with the punch. It was a challenge for me, but Jon was incredible. He really supported me with this.'

Unlike some of the actors who play male superheroes Scarlett was more than happy with her character's suit. She didn't feel constricted by it and enjoyed the reaction she got from the crew and fans of the comic Black Widow. It took her a few hours to adjust to it but after that it was fine. She had known when she signed up for the part that she would be wearing a unitard of some description, as she had seen what Black Widow wore in the comics.

In *The Avengers* Scarlett looked forward to exploring more of Black Widow's past. She was also looking forward to showing more in a spin-off film. Her character's mysterious past had to be changed from the Black Widow presented in the comics because the films were set in the modern day. Originally Black Widow had Communist connections in her backstory but these were ditched.

Scarlett did everything she could to prepare herself for playing a superhero. She confessed the Sci-Fi Movie Page: 'Black Widow is an expert in hand-to-hand combat, she's a mixed martial artist, has a dance and gymnastics background, so she combines all of these aspects into one kick-ass fighting machine, so I dedicated myself to putting in the hours, repetitions, and training with the stunt team until I felt comfortable that I could sell each particular move.

'I'm very sensitive about when you see an action sequence and the shot is on the back of somebody's head, and then all of the sudden it cuts and the actor gives that one dramatic pose at the end and it's obvious that it was not them in the shot before. It's the lamest thing, because you want to see the actor risking their own life, and that is part of what sells it to an audience. So that's why I worked for months to prepare and I really didn't want to be perceived as a little wuss who couldn't do it.'

DID YOU KNOW?

Whilst Scarlett was preparing to play the part of Black Widow her then hubby Ryan Reynolds was also preparing to play Deadpool and the Green Lantern. They had comics scattered all around their home.

BLADE (ERIC BROOKS)

- Appears in: *Blade* (1998), *Blade II* (2002), *Blade: Trinity* (2004)
- Powers: Half-vampire so is immune to vampire bites; enhanced senses, speed and strength, good at martial arts, always has plenty of weapons with him to kill vampires
- First comic-book appearance: July 1973

Blade is a Dhampir, which means he is half human, half vampire. His mother was attacked by a vampire whilst she was having Blade. Deacon Frost had pretended to be a doctor but he was really a vampire who attacked her when she was most vulnerable. Thankfully he was forced to leave before he could kill Blade, but his mother ended up dying from her injuries.

Once Blade is older and finds out that a vampire was behind the death of his mother, he becomes very angry and decides to hunt them. He learns from a retired vampire hunter called Whistler who teaches him all he can and looks after his weapons. Blade's mission gets more complicated when he finds out that the vampire who killed his mother is trying to turn himself into La Magra, the blood god.

Blade needs blood himself because he is part vampire but uses a special serum that means he doesn't have to kill. He rescues a doctor who has been bitten by a vampire and she starts looking at a permanent way to stop Blade needing blood.

When Blade finds Deacon he is shocked to find that his mother didn't die and is now a vampire. Deacon needs Blade's blood and has to sacrifice 12 pure-blood vampire leaders in order to raise La Magra. As Deacon begins to sacrifice them he becomes more powerful but Blade manages to fight his way to him. He kills numerous vampires, including the one who used to be his mother. He knows he can't kill Deacon the way he would normally kill a vampire so stabs him with every EDTA syringe he has. The substance inside the syringes reacts badly when they come into contact with Deacon's blood and cause his body to expand to such an extent that it explodes.

Dr Jensen still wants to find Blade a permanent cure but he tells her to just find a better serum because he wants to keep his powers so he can kill vampires.

In the second film Blade has a new enemy. The Reapers are vampires who lust for blood so much that they kill humans and vampires. They are killing people at such a rate that soon there

won't be enough to go round and they will end up killing all the vampires who aren't Reapers. Blade is forced to work alongside The Bloodpack, a team of vampires originally trained to kill him. Their task to destroy the Reapers is tough because the Reapers are a lot stronger than the average vampire and they have bone surrounding their hearts, which means only sunlight can kill them.

The vampire Eli Damaskinos, who arranges for Blade to work with his vampires, actually created the first Reaper, Jared Nomak. He wants to create a breed of vampires that can walk around in the sunlight and in order to do that he wants to dissect Blade.

In the third film, Blade becomes the hunted, as the vampires make him think a familiar is a vampire and in killing it he becomes guilty of murdering a human. The FBI arrest him and Blade is taken to a group of vampires posing as agents. He is rescued by the two leaders of the Nightstalkers, vampire hunters like him. Hannibal King and Abigail Whistler inform Blade that the vampire Danica Talos has found Drake (Dracula) and is planning to resurrect him. They need to stop him.

The Nightstalkers have created a weapon called the Daystar that has the potential to kill every vampire. It is a virus which needs Blade's blood to work to its full potential.

Blade and Abigail end up being the only Nightstalkers left as Drake has killed everyone apart from Hannibal and a girl called Zoe. They have been kidnapped and are being held in the Talos building. Blade and Abigail rush there and manage to free their friends, and kill their vampire captors. Blade uses the Daystar to kill Drake but before he dies Drake tells him that the vampire race will survive because of Blade. He thinks that one day Blade won't be able to hold back his vampire desires.

The actor chosen to play Blade in all three movies was Wesley Snipes. He was sent to prison in 2008 for tax evasion but was allowed out on bail while he appealed against his sentence. He would love to make a *Blade 4* in the future.

THE BLOB (FREDDIE DUKES)

⚜ Appears in: *X-Men Origins: Wolverine* (2009)

⚜ Powers: Super-strong and extremely fat, which means that punches don't hurt him and even bullets bounce off him

⚜ First comic-book appearance: January 1964

The Blob's other name is Fred Dukes. He is a mutant and was a member of Team X, but once they went their separate ways he started to eat more and more. Soon he lost his muscular physique and gained so much weight that he was virtually unrecognisable. His former Team X buddy John Wraith decides to help him and turn him into a boxer.

Logan (Wolverine) turns up whilst Dukes is training, wanting to know where his brother is. He is shocked to see how much weight his former comrade has put on and wants to question him. John Wraith warns him to not poke fun at Dukes' larger size but after Dukes mistakenly thinks Logan called him 'blob' they start fighting. Logan thinks he will beat Dukes no problem but he is strongly mistaken. He is so fat that Logan's punches don't do anything to him and the big man is able to knock him to the floor easily. Eventually Logan is able to win and finds out the truth – his brother is working with William Stryker. They are abducting mutants and performing experiments on them.

The Blob was played by Kevin Durand in *X-Men Origins: Wolverine*. He isn't a big guy so had to have a special scan done so that a fat suit could be made for him. He had wanted to be in an X-Men movie since watching the first film, so being cast as the Blob was a dream come true.

BOLT (CHRIS BRADLEY)

Appears in: *X-Men Origins: Wolverine* (2009)

Powers: Controls electricity, can create electricity fields

First comic-book appearance: October 1995

Dominic Monaghan plays Bolt/Chris Bradley in *X-Men Origins: Wolverine*. Bolt was a member of Team X but decided to join a circus once they disbanded. He is a mutant and he has the ability to control electricity. When he was in Team X he was the one in charge of flying the plane. He was hunted down by Victor Creed who killed him in his circus trailer. The nearby town went into blackout afterwards, which shows his power over electricity was immense.

Dominic is most famous for playing Charlie Pace in *Lost* and Merry in *The Lord of the Rings*. During the *X-Men Origins: Wolverine* promotion tour he was asked by *Inked Magazine* whether he was a comic-book fan. He said: 'Yeah, I got into comics through becoming friends with Elijah Wood (his co-star from *The Lord of the Rings*). In New Zealand, he and I would talk about comics. I was more into English comics and he was more into your classic American comics – your Batmans, your Spider-Mans, your Incredible Hulks. Since then I kind of got more interested in American comics.

'I obviously read a lot of Frank Miller stuff and Grant Morrison stuff... and *Y: The Last Man* and *Sandman* and *Hellboy* and stuff like that. I don't think *X-Men* was my favourite comic, but it was certainly one that I'd read and was interested in. I like the more pulp fiction type stuff – slightly crazy, weird stuff. I read a great Japanese horror comic called *Spiral*.'

Dominic's fans were a bit disappointed that Bolt didn't have much time on screen as they felt that Dominic was unable to show his full acting potential. They still thought he did well, though, in the few scenes that he was in.

BUCKY BARNES

Appears in: *Captain America: The First Avenger* (2011)

Powers: Knife-thrower, martial arts skills, cybernetic left arm which can shoot electric bolts of energy at his opponents

First comic-book appearance: March 1941

Bucky Barnes is Captain America's sidekick. His full name is James Buchanan Barnes but he goes by the name Bucky. The pair are good friends and could easily be mistaken for brothers because they are so close. They are both orphans, so consider each other family. They have grown up together but their relationship changes once Steve Rogers transforms into Captain America.

The role of Bucky went to *Gossip Girl* actor Sebastian Stan but he wasn't a huge comic-book fan in the beginning. In fact, he decided to research the role by watching war documentaries instead of studying comics like most actors do when they are given the role of a superhero. He wanted to know what it would have been like for a boy of Bucky's age to fight in the Second World War.

Originally Sebastian had wanted to play Captain America but he was glad when he got the part of Bucky. He explained the whole casting process to Eric Ditzian from MTV: 'It was interesting, because I was in Germany, so I was making tapes [for an audition]. One thing about living in New York is I always end up making tapes... Anyway, I was in Germany and I made a tape before I left New York in early January, and then I made about two or three other ones from Germany. I got a good response. I'm originally from Romania, and after I finished *Apparition*, I was going to go to Romania, but I had this feeling that I needed to go to LA. And thank God I did, because I went into the room with the guys – at the time, I was auditioning for the actual Captain America role – so I screen-tested for that role.

'Usually with screen tests you can be very nervous, the stakes are high. But this one was actually really chilled out. I think a lot of that had to do with [director] Joe Johnston, because he brings such a good atmosphere on set. I felt very calm. I wasn't nervous. I felt like, for four or five hours, I was just playing. It was fun. Kevin Feige and Stephen Broussard over at Marvel asked me to sit down with them and they talked about the comics and Bucky and his entire arc [storyline], and I was really attracted to that. I thought "there's a lot to play with," so I was very happy.'

He enjoyed doing the stunts and action scenes but admits that it was hard work. Lots of these were done with a green screen and so he didn't have a clear idea of what was going on. This usually involves actors performing in front of a green screen while the background is added in by a special effects department – so he had to try and imagine what it would look like.

C IS FOR...

CAPTAIN AMERICA (STEVE ROGERS)

✦ Appears in: *Captain America: The First Avenger* (2011), *The Avengers* (2012)

✦ Powers: Super-strength, stamina, agility, expert soldier abilities, martial arts master, never tires

✦ First comic-book appearance: March 1941

The actor chosen to play Steve Rogers and Captain America was American actor Chris Evans. He isn't a stranger to playing superheroes as he was the Human Torch (Johnny Storm) in the two Fantastic Four films. Chris also appeared in the films *Scott Pilgrim Vs. The World* and *The Losers*, which are both based on comic-book series.

In *Captain America: The First Avenger* we get to see what Steve Rogers was like before he becomes a superhero. It is 1942 and he wants to fight for the USA against the Nazis but he can't because he isn't strong enough. He is a sickly lad but this all changes when he volunteers for Project: Rebirth. They inject him with a super-soldier serum that turns him into Captain America. He fights in the war, his big opponent being Red Skull, one of Hitler's top men.

Initially, Chris Evans wasn't sure whether he wanted to commit to playing Captain America just in case the film didn't do well but a friend convinced him that he should go for it. He had to think long and hard about it because signing to play Steve Rogers in *Captain America: The First Avenger* meant committing to playing him in future films too. Marvel didn't want him to play him in just one film; they signed him for several more.

DID YOU KNOW?

Chris never auditioned for the part but the director Joe Johnston thought he would make a perfect Steve Rogers and Marvel agreed. They showed him round the art department so he could see what they were trying to do visually and offered him the part. He didn't make things easy for them – he turned them down three times before agreeing.

Chris has a lot of love for Steve and Captain America, and this shows in the interviews he does. He talked about how he played them to *Wizard* magazine in December 2010. He said: 'As far as the physicality goes, that comes from the serum, and I think special effects will help me carry the load. As far as who he is as a man, the reason he's chosen for this experiment is because he has a pure heart. It's the morality, the nobility. He's a real redeeming character to play; it's exciting to think of playing him.

'I actually have a friend of mine who I'm modelling the

character after. This guy is actually an Eagle Scout; he's one of those guys who stayed in the Boy Scouts all the way until he was 18. He's just a good human being. He does the right things, he's open, he's honest, he's sincere, he's selfless. It's something that I think everyone aspires to. A lot of the time I play characters who don't have any redeeming quality [laughs].'

Filming *Captain America: The First Avenger* was fun but Chris hardly had a minute to himself before he had to start shooting *The Avengers*. He had to put his social life and personal interests on hold for months at a time. He wanted to make sure that he did a good job too as he could be playing Captain America for the next decade if everything goes to plan. If he'd messed up and the fans hated him then the whole Captain America character could have been shelved or another actor brought in.

Chris is staying very quiet about the *The Avengers* film plot and admits it's a 'blind challenge' because he doesn't know what's going to happen – he just knows it will be good.

COLOSSUS (PETER RASPUTIN)

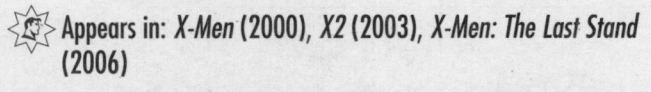 Appears in: *X-Men* (2000), *X2* (2003), *X-Men: The Last Stand* (2006)

Powers: Ability to change his body into a steel-like metal, which gives him super-strength and makes attacking him difficult

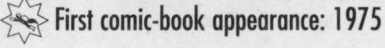 First comic-book appearance: 1975

Colossus is a mutant who is arguably the strongest of all the X-Men as he has the ability to transform his whole body into metal. In the comics he was originally from Russia, but he isn't in the films.

In the first film he was shown sketching in one scene, but that was it. In *X2* Colossus had a slightly larger role to play, but only just.

When William Stryker attacks the school a young mutant called Siryn raises the alarm. She uses her 'sonic scream' but ends up being knocked out. Thankfully Colossus comes to the rescue and helps Siryn and other students to safety. Colossus shows great bravery when he offers to stay and fight but Wolverine tells him to go.

Twilight actor Daniel Cudmore played Colossus in *X2* and in the next film *X-Men: The Last Stand*. He is a huge man, and at 6ft 7 he makes most people look tiny. He wasn't the only tall cast member, though: Hugh Jackman who plays Wolverine is 6ft 4!

In the third film we get to see Colossus's strength as he trains in the Danger Room with Wolverine. He is expected to fight the simulation of a Sentinel (a robot). As their training session draws to a close he picks up Wolverine and throws him at the Sentinel, beheading it. In the film we also learn that Rogue can use her absorption powers on him. Later, during the battle Beast is able to inject Magneto with the mutant cure because he is momentarily distracted when Colossus picks up Wolverine and launches him at the Brotherhood leader.

It is thought that Daniel will be playing Colossus in the *Deadpool* film, which is set to come out in 2014.

DID YOU KNOW?

It's down to an old ankle injury that Daniel took up acting. Originally he had planned to concentrate on football and other sports but after breaking his ankle he kept picking up injuries, so had to give up. He thought he would give acting a go and the rest is history!

Daniel was asked by website *Rock-Bottom* during an interview how he got the role of Colossus. He said: 'It was when I just started auditioning. I only had one commercial under my belt...just small things...then they had a big "cattle call" for anyone over 6ft 3, that's big, had dark hair...anyone that

resembled the character. They looked all over the place – LA, Toronto, and Vancouver...so I just went out for that, and I ended up getting called back. I remember they gave me seven call backs, and I eventually got the job.'

They also asked him whether he was a big X-Men fan. He confirmed he was: 'I never really read the comic books, but I always watched the cartoon,' he said. 'It really sucked because when I was young it was on at 3 o'clock – and my house was right on top of a hill, and the school was right at the bottom...it was probably about two miles long and pretty steep. So I used to run home and I'd get there with 15 minutes left and I'd catch the end of everything.'

CYCLOPS (SCOTT SUMMERS)

 Appears in: *X-Men* (2000), *X2* (2003), *X-Men: The Last Stand* (2006), *X-Men Origins: Wolverine* (2009)

Powers: Optic blasts

First comic-book appearance: September 1963

Cyclops is a mutant who has the power to absorb energy from the sun and blast rays from his eyes. He can't control his power so wears a special visor over his eyes – which results in him taking the name Cyclops.

In the first film Cyclops is teaching at the Xavier Institute for Higher Learning and is dating fellow mutant Jean Grey. He joins Storm in rescuing Wolverine and Rogue who have been attacked by Sabretooth. The two new mutants are welcomed into the fold but Cyclops starts to have a problem with Wolverine when he sees how the newcomer behaves around Jean Grey. He feels threatened because he thinks Wolverine could steal her from him.

Cyclops ends up battling Sabretooth again when he goes with Storm to look for Rogue after she runs away. This time Sabretooth is joined by Toad, a fellow member of the Brotherhood. Rogue steps in to help Storm when Sabretooth attacks her but this allows Toad to remove Cyclops' visor with his tongue. The train station is full of people who run for cover when Cyclops' beam destroys the roof. Cyclops and Storm fail to reach Rogue and she is captured by Magneto.

Cyclops and Storm are joined by Jean and Wolverine, and together they plan how to rescue her. Things take a turn for the worse when Professor X is poisoned whilst trying to see where Rogue is by using his Cerebro device. Cyclops leads the rescue team to the Statue of Liberty but he ends up getting trapped in a cage by Toad. He then uses his power beam to blast his way out and save Jean who has Toad's slime on her face, preventing her from breathing. They come under attack again and Cyclops blasts Sabretooth in the head before taking care of Magneto.

In *X2* Cyclops still hates Wolverine. Jean thinks that something terrible is about to happen but Cyclops tells her he will protect her. He goes with Professor X to see Magneto in his cell but waits outside to let the two leaders talk to each other. He is ambushed by Yuriko Oyama (Lady Deathstrike) and her henchmen. Knowing that Professor X could be in deep trouble he goes to blast open the cell door but is knocked unconscious by Yuriko. Strykur is thrilled to have captured both Cyclops and Professor X. He brainwashes Cyclops and when the X-Men arrive to try and free Professor X, he ends up fighting against the woman he loves, Jean.

As Cyclops and Jean fight they cause a crack to form in the dam. Once Cyclops regains control of his himself and realises what he has done he helps Jean to the X-Jet. She decides to go back and hold back the water so that the other X-Men can escape.

In the *The Last Stand*, Cyclops is constantly getting telepathic messages from Jean, even though she is dead. He returns to the

Alkali Lake where she died and unleashes his optic blasts on the water. This causes Jean to appear from the lake and they embrace. As they kiss, Jean removes Cyclops' visor and controls his optic blasts. He has never been able to control them himself, which shows how powerful she has become. Cyclops' face distorts as they kiss. Back at the X-Mansion Professor X senses that Cyclops is dead and sends Wolverine and Storm to the lake. They find no sign of their friend apart from his visor and discover Jean unconscious.

In *X-Men Origins: Wolverine* we meet a younger Cyclops who is constantly being told off for wearing sunglasses in class. He is kidnapped by Victor for his powers and becomes a prisoner until Wolverine rescues him and the other young mutant captives. He uses his eye blasts during the escape, with the help of Emma Frost who tells him where to aim them. He is telepathically guided by Professor X so that he can lead them out to safety and goes with Professor X in his helicopter to the school.

In the *X-Men*, *X2* and *X-Men: The Last Stand* movies he was played by James Marsden. James also played Lois Lane's fiancé Richard White in *Superman Returns*.

He told Cinema Source he does get recognised in the street: 'I do have someone occasionally yell, "Cyclops", and I turn. But fans have been really pleasant, in my experience. They've been really happy with the movies. It just makes me feel good that I did something right.'

Australian actor Tim Pocock took over from James to play Cyclops in *X-Men Origins: Wolverine*.

D IS FOR...

DAREDEVIL (MATT MURDOCK)

- Appears in: *Daredevil* (2003)
- Powers: Radar sense, heightened senses, trained fighter whose weapon of choice is his billy club
- First comic-book appearance: April 1964

Matt Murdock is a blind lawyer who might not be able to see but his other senses are magnified. Matt hasn't always been blind. He lost his sight as a young boy when a forklift truck accidentally punctured a barrel full of toxic waste as he was passing and some of it went into his eyes. Shortly afterwards his boxer father was murdered by Wilson 'Kingpin' Fisk, on orders given to him by his gangster boss Fallon. Matt's father was killed because he refused to throw a fight.

Now Matt is an adult he works in the courtroom during the day, fighting for the underdogs, but at night he becomes the superhero Daredevil. The only person to know of his secret identity is his priest.

Matt meets Elektra, the daughter of Nikolas Natchios, and they start dating. Elektra doesn't know it but her businessman father is part of the criminal underworld. He has decided to change, though, and no longer wants to work with Kingpin. The mob boss isn't at all pleased when he hears Nikolas's news. His secret identity is well hidden but a journalist called Ben Urich is trying to discover who Kingpin is. This gives Kingpin an idea – he will set Nikolas up as Kingpin to take the heat off himself.

Nikolas starts to fear for his life and plans to leave town with Elektra. Before they can escape they are both attacked by Bullseye, who has been sent by Kingpin to kill them both. Bullseye uses Daredevil's billy club to stab Nikolas, which makes Elektra think that Daredevil killed her father. She doesn't realise that Matt is Daredevil.

Later, Daredevil goes on the hunt for Bullseye but ends up being attacked by Elektra and having to fight her. He doesn't want to but has no choice. She manages to unmask him during the fight; she can't believe the man she has been dating is Daredevil. Bullseye arrives and Elektra realises that he is the real murderer. They fight but Bullseye stabs her with one of her sai weapons. He throws her from a rooftop, finds a red rose in his pocket and wipes it on his forehead before throwing it next to her body.

Daredevil can't do anything to help and has to watch as Elektra passes away. He chases after Bullseye to a church where they fight. Bullseye cleverly uses the bells and parts of the church's organ to distract Daredevil who can't cope with loud noises. He is stumped when he runs out of shurikens (throwing stars) and ends up breaking a stained glass window so he can use the shards of glass as a weapon. He tosses them at Daredevil but

they miss him as he does continuous back flips. They carry on fighting but Daredevil hears a bullet being fired by a SWAT sniper and manages to move Bullseye's arm so that the bullet goes through both his hands. Bullseye is no match for Daredevil without the ability to throw things and Daredevil throws him through a window.

During the fight Bullseye revealed that Wilson Fisk is Kingpin – the man who murdered Matt's dad. As soon as Daredevil defeats Bullseye he goes on the hunt for him, finding him in his office. Kingpin might be overweight, but you can't be a mobster boss without having the ability to fight. He attacks Daredevil who is carrying injuries from his earlier battle with Bullseye. He throws Daredevil against the window, the ceiling and the wall, which makes his head spin. Kingpin doesn't regret killing Matt's dad or ordering Bullseye to kill Elektra because he sees it as just 'business'. Daredevil lies on the floor and Kingpin unmasks him. Seeing that the blind lawyer is Daredevil makes Kingpin laugh. Daredevil's senses are impaired so he bursts a decorative water pipe that runs throughout Kingpin's office. Suddenly he can 'see' again as the water hits Kingpin, allowing him to accurately pinpoint where he is. Daredevil ends up standing over a powerless Kingpin. He could kill him but he would much rather see him go to prison. They hear police sirens and Kingpin wrongly assumes that the police are coming to arrest his intruder. Daredevil explains that they are coming for Kingpin because his cover has been blown. Kingpin laughs and says he'll be released from prison, but Daredevil replies that he will be waiting for him. Kingpin knows that Daredevil is Matt so threatens to tell people but Daredevil doesn't think he will, otherwise he would have to admit that he was 'beaten by a blind man'.

Matt/Daredevil was supposed to feature in the movie *Elektra* but the scene was cut and only appears in the Director's Cut version.

The actor originally chosen to play Daredevil was Vin Diesel but he turned down the part because he was already signed up to play Xander Cage in the action film *xXx*. Ben Affleck was then cast instead. He was really enthusiastic about playing Daredevil because it was his favourite comic when he was a boy. He read all the *Daredevil* comics before shooting the film and revealed to MTV that he shared his passion for Daredevil with the writer/director Mark Steven Johnson: 'Not only do we both love the comic, but we love the same issues, particularly the Frank Miller run…we both felt that it was really important to at least maintain the integrity of that tone, that story-line and those characters. We figured that if we were going to fail, we'd fail emulating that particular thing.

'Sometimes [filmmakers] take the comic books and they think, "OK, we are going to turn it into a movie, but we are going to change everything." We were both such big fans of it, we were like, "Why change it? Let's just do it and keep it what it is."'

During a *Daredevil* press conference in Los Angeles Ben was asked by a journalist what 'sensitivity' he had to take to prepare to portray a blind character. He replied: 'It's kind of misleading. In a way, he is blind, yes, but because he's able to cobble together a mosaic impression of everything around him based on his other heightened senses, he is able to navigate the world… It's kind of a sonar, which will be represented in the movie with this really cool series of effects that Mark created, this kind of shadow world. He sees things, but he can't really see texture. He knows where things are, but he still has to fold his bills the way a regular blind man folds his bills so he doesn't get a one-dollar and a five-dollar bill confused. He still has to read Braille text to find his clothes. So Mark tried to create a combination of the vulnerability of his [DISABILIM], with the extra abilities…'

He also explained how much the character is based on the one in the comics: 'As far as the genre of comic-book movies

goes, this one is definitely aiming more towards the character in the story. So the challenge is to make it honest and believable.'

To make sure that Ben acted like a blind man and didn't maintain eye contact with anyone, he was given special contact lenses to wear that made his vision blurred. He also spent time with Tom Sullivan, a blind actor, singer, author and producer. Tom is a very inspirational man who has climbed Mount Everest, plays golf, bungee jumps… and believes that you shouldn't let your disability hold you back.

DID YOU KNOW?

Ben started dating Jennifer Garner who played Elektra shortly after he filmed his scene for her film. They got married in 2005 and now have two daughters together, Violet and Seraphina.

DARWIN (ARMANDO MUNOZ)

Appears in: *X-Men: First Class* (2011)

Powers: Reactive evolution

First comic-book appearance: February 2006

Darwin is a mutant who is constantly evolving so that he has the right physicality for any situation he is placed in. The actor chosen to play him was Edi Gathegi who is most famous for playing the vampire Laurent in the *Twilight Saga* films. He did a lot of kickboxing and training in the gym to make sure he was physically fit enough to play Darwin.

E IS FOR...

EMMA FROST

- Appears in: *X-Men Origins: Wolverine* (2009), *X-Men: First Class* (2011)

- Powers: Telepathy, ability to turn her body into diamond, psionic abilities, telekinetic powers

- First comic-book appearance: January 1980

Emma Frost is a mutant who can harden her skin to be like diamonds, allowing her to act as a shield and prevent bullets making an impact. She also goes by the name White Queen and her sister is Kayla Silverfox.

Emma was a prisoner in William Stryker's Weapons X Facility until Wolverine helped her and the other captive mutants to escape. She was invited by Professor X to join his school.

In *X-Men Origins: Wolverine,* Tahyna Tozzi played Emma, but she was replaced by January Jones for the *X-Men: First Class* film. January is most famous for playing Betty Draper in the TV drama series *Mad Men.*

DID YOU KNOW?

January dated Ashton Kutcher when she first moved to Los Angeles dreaming she would become an actress, but she says he wasn't very supportive and that made her try even harder.

F IS FOR...

FANTASTIC FOUR

- Appears in: *Fantastic Four* (2005), *Fantastic Four: Rise of the Silver Surfer* (2007)
- Powers: Various
- First comic-book appearance: November 1961

The Fantastic Four are four people who ended up with extraordinary powers after coming into contact with a cosmic energy cloud. They are scientist Reed Richards (Mr Fantastic), researcher Susan Storm (Invisible Woman), astronaut Johnny Storm (Human Torch) and fellow astronaut Ben Grimm (The Thing).

In the first *Fantastic Four* film they gain their powers and have to defeat Doctor Doom. In the second film they are up against the Silver Surfer, Doctor Doom and Galactus. Both films did

well in the box office but critics didn't rate them. In 2009 it was announced that the 20th Century Fox studio were rebooting *Fantastic Four*, so there will be at least one more film, due to be released in 2013. It's thought that the movie will take a new direction so new actors are expected to play the Fantastic Four. The Thing will probably be CGI (computer-generated), rather than having an actor wearing a suit as in the first two movies.

FLASH

Appears in: *The Flash* TV series (1990–1991)
Powers: Extremely fast, ability to pass through objects
First comic-book appearance: January 1940

Flash is a superhero who goes by the name The Scarlet Speedster and has the ability to run as fast as the speed of light. He can pass through objects by getting his molecules to vibrate. There have been three Flashes: Jay Garrick, Barry Allen and Wally West.

In *The Flash* TV series the lead character was based on both Barry and Wally from the comics. Barry was a forensic scientist and in the series he did have a relationship with Iris although it didn't last as long as it did in the comics. In the series his biggest enemies were the Trickster, Captain Cold and Mirror Master. The actor chosen to play Flash was John Wesley Shipp.

Warner Bros want to bring out a Flash movie in the next few years and have hired the *Green Lantern* writers to work on a treatment. They will be presenting Barry Allen as the Flash in the film.

G IS FOR...

GAMBIT (REMY LEBEAU)

⭐ Appears in: *X-Men Origins: Wolverine* (2009)
⭐ Powers: Ability to charge objects so they explode
⭐ First comic-book appearance: August 1990

Gambit is a mutant who has the ability to manipulate kinetic energy so that he can make any object he touches explode on impact. He is also highly skilled at card throwing and one-on-one combat. His weapon of choice is his staff. He managed to escape from Stryker's laboratory, 'The Island', which is no mean feat.

Wolverine approaches Gambit in the hope that he will tell him where The Island is but Gambit thinks it is a setup and that Wolverine has been sent to take him back there. He notices the

dog tags that Wolverine wears and remarks that the man who kidnapped him last time wore similar tags. He raises his pack of cards into the air and fires the cards at Wolverine with such force that he is sent flying backwards, through a wall and into an alleyway.

Victor arrives and battles with Wolverine but before Wolverine has a chance to kill his brother, Gambit causes an explosion that gives Victor time to escape. Gambit still thinks that Wolverine is the bad guy and they fight again, until finally Gambit realises his mistake. He agrees to take him to The Island but says he won't be going inside with him.

The actor chosen to play Gambit was Taylor Kitsch. Taylor enjoyed putting his own twist on the character, as he explained to journalist Andrea Warner before filming started: 'I knew X-Men and I knew of Gambit, but the more I learned about him, the more I wanted to play him…he's definitely a cool cat. And there's so much room to take him and discover so many things that are a part of him, too. I'm really excited about it, and hopefully we can do a few of these.'

GHOST RIDER (JOHNNY BLAZE)

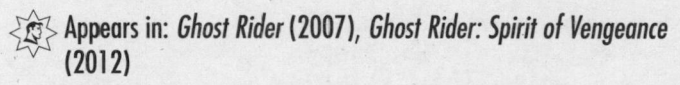 Appears in: *Ghost Rider* (2007), *Ghost Rider: Spirit of Vengeance* (2012)

 Powers: Supernatural powers, including his Penance Stare

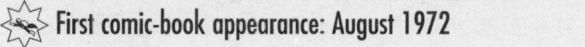 First comic-book appearance: August 1972

The Ghost Rider is a bounty hunter who collects corrupt souls for Mephistopheles.

Johnny Blaze is a motorbike stunt man in a travelling circus. He performs his act with his dad, Barton Blaze. Things are going well for them, and Johnny has a lovely girlfriend called Roxanne.

Sadly, Barton develops advanced cancer and Johnny is so desperate for his dad to survive that he sells his soul to Mephistopheles in return for his dad being cured of cancer. He wakes up in the morning to find his dad fighting fit but later that day he dies doing a stunt.

Mephistopheles took Johnny's Soul, as he only promised to cure Barton of cancer. He didn't want his Ghost Rider to be distracted and warns Johnny to not have family or friends. He tells him he will come back for him one day when he needs him. Johnny ends his relationship with Roxanne – leaving her waiting in the rain for him, crushing her dreams of them running away to be together.

Years pass and Johnny has become a famous stunt rider, taking on jumps that no one else would dare to do. He walks away from crashes that should have killed him – all the time wondering if it is his skill or because Mephistopheles is keeping him alive. On the anniversary of his dad's death he plans to do his biggest jump yet – even though his crewmates think it is mission impossible. As he leaves his dressing room he is asked whether he would do an interview – and on discovering that the journalist interviewing him will be Roxanne he agrees. It's clear he still has feelings for her, even though she brushes him off and leaves before he jumps. He sees it as a sign and after making the jump rushes out of the stadium on his bike to catch up with the van Roxanne and her cameraman are travelling in. After bringing traffic to a standstill Johnny manages to arrange a date with Roxanne that night.

He never gets the chance to show up though, because Mephistopheles finds him and tells him he has to go after Blackheart, his son. If he manages to kill/capture him Mephistopheles will give him back his soul. Johnny doesn't want to go after Blackheart but he has no choice; he transforms into the Ghost Rider!

As he searches for Blackheart he kills one of his minions, a

mugger, and some criminals that he ends up being stuck in a police cell with. Ghost Rider kills evil people who have done wrong by using his Penance Stare. When he looks someone in the eye they relive all the evil things they have done in the past and it kills them. During his journey he meets the Caretaker, an old man who recognises that he is the Ghost Rider. He works at the cemetery where Johnny's dad is buried.

After one battle with Blackheart on the top of a building, the police force and Roxanne witness him kill Abigor, one of Blackheart's henchmen. The police shoot at Ghost Rider but their bullets don't affect him. Roxanne realises that the Ghost Rider is Johnny. Blackheart notices and knows then that the way to destroy the Ghost Rider is through Roxanne.

The Caretaker explains to Johnny that long ago his predecessor was sent to San Venganza with a contract to collect 1,000 corrupt souls, but he refused to do it because he knew how much power would be given to Mephistopheles if he handed it over. He decided to hide the contract and himself – in the hope that Mephistopheles would never find them. Blackheart is searching for the contract because he wants to be more powerful that his father. The Caretaker warns Johnny that he needs to keep his distance from his friends and family because Blackheart will go after them.

Johnny rushes home but Blackheart has killed his friend and already has Roxanne. He tries to fight him but it is useless – his Penance Stare doesn't work because Blackheart doesn't have a soul. Blackheart gives him an ultimatum: he wants Johnny to get him the contract, and in return he will let Roxanne live.

Johnny goes back to the cemetery and using the Caretaker's shovel starts to dig – he thinks the contract must be buried in one of the graves. He is wrong, as the Caretaker reveals that the contract is in fact hidden in the shovel – and he is the Ghost Rider who refused to hand it over to Mephistopheles in the first place. Once he has the contract, Johnny heads out to San

SARAH OLIVER

Venganza with the Caretaker as his guide. The Caretaker gives Johnny his Ghost Rider shotgun that shoots Hellfire, and says his goodbyes.

Johnny battles with Wallow, Blackheart's last remaining henchman, before arriving at the ruins. Blackheart insists he stays in his human form otherwise he will kill Roxanne. Johnny agrees and after Blackheart throws Roxanne to one side he goes to hand over the contract. He doesn't let go of the parchment and instead turns into Ghost Rider. He battles Blackheart but as the sun appears he can't keep his Ghost Rider powers and turns back into Johnny. Meanwhile, Blackheart reads the contract and the souls of a thousand people pour out from the ruins walls and enter him. He is no longer Blackheart but the all-powerful Legion.

Roxanne wants Johnny to run away with her whilst they can but he can't because he has a job to do. He manages to get Legion to fight him in an area with more shadows. Legion goes to kill him but Roxanne shoots the Caretaker's gun at him. It quickly runs out of ammunition but Johnny asks her to throw it at him. She does, and as his hands wrap around it flames start to appear. He shoots, but although it looks like Legion has been obliterated he soon re-forms. Johnny walks to him and uses his Penance Stare – Legion has forgotten that in gaining 1,000 souls he has made himself extremely vulnerable. He quickly turns to dust.

Mephistopheles arrives and offers to give Johnny back his soul and make someone else the Ghost Rider but Johnny refuses. He vows to keep his powers and use them against Mephistopheles and to protect the innocent. Every time innocent blood is spilt he will think of his dad. Mephistopheles is furious!

The film ends with Johnny and Roxanne together under the tree where they used to meet before Johnny's dad was sick.

The actor Nicolas Cage played the older Johnny Blaze and Ghost Rider, and Matt Long played the teenage Johnny Blake. Sam Elliott played the Caretaker/Ghost Rider.

Nicolas Cage changed Johnny from the character portrayed in the comics. He didn't want to play him as someone who drinks and smokes a lot. He told the *Manila Bulletin*: 'I was concerned that this wasn't sort of your typical hero. I wanted to approach it from the point of view of someone who is beleaguered by this contract of selling his soul to the devil.

'I'm playing him more as someone who, he's made this deal and he's trying to avoid confronting it, anything he can do to keep it away from him... the stunt riding keeps him connected to his father, who's passed away. So there's a version of being able to keep that relationship going when he's jumping, because that's what his father taught him.'

He also confessed: 'Something happened to me before we shot *Ghost Rider* that made my fitness regimen more intense. I was in Africa shooting *Lord of War*, and we went to this place in the middle of the desert to shoot for about a week. But there weren't a lot of people there. And I was stuck there and I was driving home in a van, there was a cobra in the road. And I said, Let's back up; let's look at it. So we backed it up and the cobra got up and attacked my car. And I was shocked, and I never got that image out of my head. And then shortly after that, I started eating smaller portions. I stopped imbibing as much, I didn't go out as much, didn't have as many cocktails. And I just kind of worked out a lot more, and got ready for this role. So I think it had something to do with this cobra.'

DID YOU KNOW?

Nicolas Cage was once considered to play Clark Kent and Superman.

The second Ghost Rider film will be released in February 2012. *Ghost Rider: Spirit of Vengeance* sees Johnny trying to stop Mephistopheles from taking human form, protect a young boy

and save the world. Nicolas Cage will once again be playing Johnny and Ghost Rider. He must have loved being able to jump on his motorbike again.

DID YOU KNOW?

Nicolas Cage has loved Ghost Rider since he was a little boy and he even has a Ghost Rider tattoo.

He told a journalist called Fischer at *Superherohype.com*: 'As a boy I was really attracted to the monsters that were in the Marvel universe, such as the Hulk and Ghost Rider, because I couldn't understand how something so terrifying could also be good, so it appealed to whatever complexities I was feeling about life, and that paradox to me is inherently interesting.

'I would just sit in my room and stare at the covers...there's something about the iconography of the flaming skull itself, even going beyond Ghost Rider, that has been around for thousands of years, something about the flaming skull that depicts honesty. It's like there's no mask, you can't hide, and there it is, the truth, and I like that.'

GREEN HORNET (BRITT REID)

Appears in: *The Green Hornet* (2011)

Powers: None

First comic-book appearance: December 1940

Britt Reid is a lazy guy in his late twenties who still lives at home with his dad. While his dad runs one of the biggest newspapers in Los Angeles, Britt stays at home, gets drunk, goes to parties

and doesn't do much else. He lives off his dad who he's not particularly close to, but one day his dad dies from a bee sting and Britt is forced to grow up.

Britt hates the way people loved his dad and when a statue is erected he decides to have his revenge on the man who pulled the head off his action figure when he was a little boy. He manages to behead the statue but on his way back to his car he witnesses a woman being attacked. He decides to take on the robbers, which isn't his cleverest move and thankfully his driver Kato manages to beat them all.

The buzz that Britt feels after their fight makes him want to do it again and he suggests that they pose as villains so they can catch the real villains. The next day he goes into the newspaper offices that he now owns and states that they will be running a front-page story on the mystery man who vandalised his dad's statue. After the names he suggests are rejected, the board of journalists and Kato come up with the name the Green Hornet.

Britt and Kato modify their car, the Black Beauty, and set about hitting drug dens and other places criminals hang out. Britt might not be the best fighter but he has a good heart. He wants to bring down the number one gangster in Los Angeles, Benjamin Chudnofsky. He hires Lenore Case to be his assistant, and constantly asks her what she thinks Green Hornet's next move should be. She is a criminology expect and for a while it seems like both Britt and Kato have a huge crush on her.

Kato is definitely the brains of the superhero duo, even though he doesn't get the credit, often being referred to as 'the driver'. He spots that Chudnofsky is setting them up and saves Britt's life when both Chudnofsky and District Attorney Frank Scanlon try to have him killed.

Britt thinks he has recorded Scanlon admitting that he killed Britt's dad (it wasn't a bee sting after all), and that he did it because he controls the crime in Los Angeles whilst making himself look

good at the same time. Britt rushes to the newspaper offices with Kato to try and get the recording on the web before they can be silenced.

Once there they have to fight Chudnofsky and his henchmen and battle to reach the right floor in what remains of Black Beauty. As soon as he sticks the memory stick/recorder into the computer Britt discovers that he didn't record Scanlon after all. He doesn't have time to think, though, as Chudnofsky (now called Bloodnofsky) is about to kill Kato until he steps in. He manages to distract Bloodnofsky long enough for Kato to stab him in the eye with a table leg and then Britt shoots him with his own double-barrelled gun.

The SWAT team arrive and Scanlon tells them to arrest the Green Hornet – but Britt and Kato aren't going to let him get away with what he did to Britt's dad. They jump into the small section of Black Beauty that remains and drive him out of the 10th-floor office window before anyone can stop them.

They manage to escape and go to the one person who will believe what they tell her. Lenore is shocked but ultimately stands by them. Britt has been shot, and after she fails to remove the bullet they come up with a master plan.

In the morning Lenore organises a press conference at the newspaper's office. As Britt tells the waiting journalists that he is promoting experienced journalist Mike Axford to editor-in-chief, a speeding car arrives, a gun is fired by Kato, and Britt pretends to have been shot. Lenore quickly gets him away and to the hospital. In reality he was shot hours previously but they want to maintain the idea that the Green Hornet is on the run and Britt has nothing to do with him.

The film ends with Britt fixing the head back on his dad's statue and accepting that his dad wasn't the bad man he thought he was. He's going to continue to be the Green Hornet with help from Kato and Lenore.

The actor who played Britt and the Green Hornet was Seth

Rogen. This film was a long time coming as it was originally planned to come out in the 1990s. In one version of the script George Clooney was going to be playing Britt and in another Jet Li was down to be playing Kato. The film wouldn't have been half as funny if Seth hadn't played Britt – and he brought something new to the superhero movie genre.

During an interview with Collider.com, Seth, the director Michel Gondry and the producer Neal Moritz discussed how the movie wasn't based on the Green Hornet portrayed in comic books. They used the comics for inspiration but the only things that stayed the same were his name and that he pretends to be a criminal in order to catch criminals.

Michel confided: 'What is important to say is that the Green Hornet has so many forms. It was a comic. Then it was on television and then you have Bruce Lee. We had to digest all of that to find what would be our version of the Green Hornet. As a director I was thinking [of making] a movie before it was asked to be a film. And as well, the notion of Kato has evolved so much over the years. [He was] supposed to be Japanese and then during WWII, but because of the war they had to change character so he was not Japanese. He was Filipino and then he was Chinese...we respect that but we had to bring it to a place that it would fit now.'

GREEN LANTERN (HAL JORDAN)

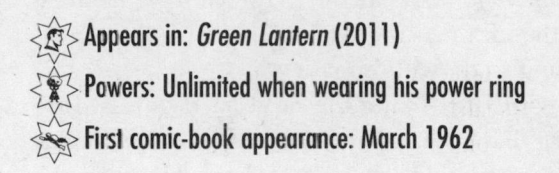

Appears in: *Green Lantern* (2011)

Powers: Unlimited when wearing his power ring

First comic-book appearance: March 1962

Hal Jordan is an overconfident but highly skilled test pilot. His love interest Carol Ferris is a fellow pilot and the vice-president

of Ferris Aircraft. Hal witnessed his dad die and this has shaped the adult he has become.

He manages to crash his plane during one exercise and shortly afterwards witnesses what looks like an alien spaceship crash landing. Inside is a dying Green Lantern who hands Hal his ring and tells him that the ring has chosen him to be a member of the Green Lantern Corps. Their mission is to defend justice and peace in the galaxies. Each member of the group has superpowers that help them with their task thanks to the special rings they wear. Hal is the first human ever to have been chosen.

Hal can't help but show his human nature and the fact that he gets scared, even though Green Lanterns are supposed to be fearless. When they face their toughest enemy yet, Parallax, it is down to Hal to save them, and Earth, from destruction.

The actor chosen to play Hal and Green Lantern was Ryan Reynolds. He had already proved his ability to play a character with superpowers from playing Deadpool in *X-Men Origins: Wolverine*. He was thrilled to secure the part because he loved the character as soon as he started talking to the director Martin Campbell about the film. Other actors had been interested too: *Star Trek*'s Chris Pine, *Clash of the Titans*' Sam Worthington and musician/actor Justin Timberlake.

DID YOU KNOW?
Ryan had to do two screen tests to prove he was the right man for the job.

Even putting on the Green Lantern costume was a big event for Ryan because he realised how much his life was going to change. He would be playing the Green Lantern for several films and it would become the part he would be most famous for playing.

A journalist from Collider.com asked Ryan back in July 2010

what it is that makes the Green Lantern character so interesting. He replied: 'Unlike many of the comic books, there's such a vast universe to this character and his contemporaries. For the most part, this is an Origins story and I was able to focus a little on *Secret Origins* [the comic-book series], but our script is a much more in-depth interpretation of that basic storyline.

'Geoff Johns described this thing as a version of *Star Wars* in the DC universe, and I think that was a pretty apt description. You have so much you can mine out of this, with these comics and this character. Any time you're dealing with a guy who has something unbelievable and insurmountable to overcome, it makes for an interesting story. As an actor, it's an interesting and excellent [Role] to get an opportunity to play. This guy has a distinct starting point. He's a bit of a fractured human being, having seen his father die. Later in life, he's cocky and aimless. It's this extraordinary power bestowed on him that sets him on a humbling path.'

Ryan also chatted about his Green Lantern mask, and revealed a behind-the-scenes secret. He said: 'I have one little anecdote I haven't mentioned yet. There was a *Cinderella* element to it. The FX house has this thing called life casts that you can build a prosthetic around. The FX house that was asked to make the Green Lantern mask had no idea who was auditioning, but they arbitrarily chose my head from their vast catalogues of heads. So, when I showed up, my mask fit a little better than someone else's would have fit.'

Ryan wasn't the only Green Lantern to be cast. Mark Strong was given the role of Hal's teacher and fellow Green Lantern member, Thaal Sinestro.

He explained to *USA Today*: 'The film closely follows the early comics. Sinestro starts out as Hal Jordan's mentor, slightly suspicious and not sure of him because obviously Hal is the first human being who's made into a Green Lantern. He's certainly very strict and certainly unsure of the wisdom of Hal becoming a Green Lantern.

'[Sinestro] is a military guy but isn't immediately bad. It's the kind of person he is that lends himself to becoming bad over the course of the comics being written, but initially he's quite a heroic figure.'

Sinestro has red skin and a moustache, making him look rather evil. He'll no doubt turn out to be a bit of a villain in future Green Lantern films.

H IS FOR...

HANCOCK

⚜ Appears in: *Hancock* (2008)

⚜ Powers: super-strength, ability to fly, immortality

⚜ First comic-book appearance: n/a

Hancock is a superhero like no other. He saves people but in the process causes millions of pounds' worth of damage. He might be able to fly and have super-strength as one of his abilities, but because he drinks this affects him in a big way. He is immortal but he can't remember what happened to him in the past – he can remember the last 80 years but nothing more.

After saving Ray, a man who vows to change the public's opinion of him, Hancock discovers that Ray's wife Mary is a superhero too. In fact they are a 'pair' and spent 3,000 years

together until Hancock got seriously injured and Mary had to leave him. Whenever they are close to one another they lose their powers and so Mary saved his life that day 80 years ago.

In the present day they fight and Hancock ends up getting shot after tackling some thieves. Bullets wouldn't normally affect him but because he is close to Mary again they do. He ends up in hospital and a trio of criminals arrive to attack him whilst he's injured. Hancock tries to fight back and manages to stop two of them; Mary gets shot in the process but thankfully Ray manages to kill the last of the thieves. Mary is in such a bad way that Hancock knows he must get as far away from her as possible so she can get her superpowers back and heal.

The actor who played Hancock was Will Smith. *Hancock 2* is due to be released in 2013. Fans are excited to see what will happen next for Hancock and Mary.

HARRY OSBORN

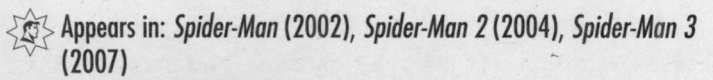 Appears in: *Spider-Man* (2002), *Spider-Man 2* (2004), *Spider-Man 3* (2007)

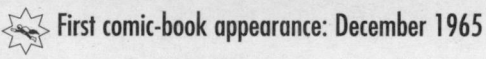 Powers: When he becomes the New Goblin he has advanced weaponry, pumpkin bombs and goblin glider

First comic-book appearance: December 1965

Harry Osborn is Peter Parker's best friend. He is extremely wealthy thanks to his dad Norman being the CEO of his own company, Oscorp. Oscorp manufactures chemicals and Norman wants them to supply chemical weapons to the US army. His mum died when he was young and Norman isn't the most loving of dads. He doesn't give Harry much attention and seems more interested in Peter because he is very intelligent and excels at science.

Harry and Peter go on a school field trip to a genetics lab and during their visit Peter is bitten by a genetically modified spider. Peter develops spider-like abilities but he doesn't tell Harry. He keeps the fact that he can jump with ease from one building to the next and that he can shoot webbing from his wrists a secret. When he decides to take on the secret identity of Spider-Man and fight crime he doesn't let his friend know.

Meanwhile, Harry's dad decides to test the weapons that he wants to sell to the army on himself, and the special serum he takes leaves him with a split personality. He becomes the Green Goblin but Harry has no idea. After his dad nearly kills Peter's Aunt May because Peter won't join forces with him, Harry visits the hospital and sees Peter and Mary Jane holding hands. When he mentions it to his dad he unwittingly puts Mary Jane at risk, as the Green Goblin now knows Spider-Man's weak spot.

Thankfully Spider-Man manages to save Mary Jane but during his battle with the Green Goblin he is almost killed when the Green Goblin takes off his mask and reveals that he is Norman, and activates his glider behind Spider-Man. As he presses the button to make it fly forwards Spider-Man senses it and manages to jump at just the right time. The glider smashes into the Green Goblin, its sharp spikes ripping into his suit. In his final words he asks Spider-Man to not tell Harry that he was the Green Goblin.

Later, Peter (dressed as Spider-Man) carries Norman's battered body back to his mansion. He doesn't know it but Harry sees him. From that moment on he thinks that Spider-Man killed his dad. He tells Peter at the funeral that he plans to kill Spider-Man, not realising that Peter is Spider-Man.

In the second film we see Harry has become the CEO of Oscorp. He hires a world-renowned scientist called Otto Octavius to come and work for him. When an experiment Otto performs goes wrong and several robotic arms with artificial intelligence are fused with his spine he becomes Doctor Octopus.

During a night out Harry has too much to drink and hits Peter; he is still angry about what happened to his dad and still blames Spider-Man. He is jealous of the relationship Peter had with his dad and he is sick of the way Peter always defends Spider-Man.

Harry does a deal with Doctor Octopus as he wants Spider-Man dead and Octopus needs tritium for his experimental reactor. He tells Octopus that Peter is the man who will be able to get him access to Spider-Man, not caring about his friend's safety. Octopus tells Peter that he wants Spider-Man to meet him at the Westside Tower at 3 o'clock or he will 'peel the flesh' off Mary Jane. Peter can't refuse and they end up fighting all over New York before Peter is forced to save people on a runaway train. It takes all of his energy so he collapses and a delighted Octopus is able to deliver him to Harry.

Harry unmasks him and is horrified to find that his best friend is Spider-Man, the person he hates most in the whole world. Peter quickly explains that he needs to stop Octopus because he has Mary Jane and because of the damage his finished reactor could do. Harry lets him go.

Later, Harry sees a vision of his dad in a mirror, telling him to avenge his death. He won't do it and to get rid of his dad's face he smashes the mirror. He finds a room he never knew existed and inside sees all the Green Goblin's weaponry and the dangerous serum. He knows his dad's secret – he was the Green Goblin!

In the third film, Harry becomes the New Goblin, using his dad's equipment to fly after Spider-Man and attack him. He ends up getting knocked out and suffers from temporary amnesia. He sees his dad in a vision again and then decides to ruin Peter's relationship with Mary Jane.

He is given the perfect opportunity when Mary Jane confides in him that Peter has changed. The symbiote that has attached itself to Peter's Spider-Man costume has transformed him into a

different person who is no longer kind and caring but arrogant and self-obsessed. Mary Jane's acting career had taken a nosedive and she can't talk to Peter about how low she is feeling. She talks to Harry instead and he tells her to break it off with Peter. She does, telling him that she is in love with someone else. He is shocked when Harry turns up when Mary Jane has gone to reveal that he is her mystery man. He attacks him and the 'evil' side of Peter emerges thanks to his new suit. He tells Harry his dad never loved him and Harry throws one of his pumpkin bombs at him, only for Peter to use a web to stop it and throw it back at him. The bomb scars the side of Harry's face.

When Venom and the Sandman kidnap Mary Jane, Peter realises that he will need help to rescue her, so goes to Harry who initially refuses because he still thinks he killed his dad. Thankfully, the family butler is able to put him straight and explains what really happened. He cleaned Norman's wounds on the night he died and it was his own glider that killed him, not Spider-Man.

Harry now realises that Peter isn't a murderer and goes with him to the building site to help. Harry tries to control the Sandman whilst Spider-Man fights Venom. Harry ends up sacrificing himself when Venom tries to kill Spider-Man with Harry's glider. The glider stabs him in the chest, just like the glider had done to his dad during his fight with Spider-Man.

After Spider-Man has defeated Venom with one of Harry's bombs and the Sandman disappears he rushes to Harry's side. Mary Jane comforts Harry as he slips away and both Harry and Peter apologise for what they have done in the past. Harry forgives Peter for his dad's death.

The actor who played Harry and the New Goblin in all three films was James Franco. He talked to journalist Shelia Roberts about how he got the part and why Harry and Peter are so similar: 'Well, people bring up the fact that I auditioned for Peter Parker and I tested and it was huge test. It must have been

thousands of dollars just for this test,' he said. 'There were cranes and sets and they kept me waiting about six weeks. And then Tobey got the role. Nobody believes me when I say that I think he's perfect for the role. I think he has done a better job than I would do in that role. But after the test, after Tobey got it, I guess Sam [Raimi, the director] and I got along well enough that he wanted me in the movie.

'And as far as I know he didn't audition anybody else for Harry and he just called me up and asked me if I wanted to play that role. Obviously it's a smaller role, but they've given me a lot to do in that role. It's one of the more dramatic parts. He goes through a lot in these films. I've been very happy with it.'

He also spoke about the similarities between the two characters: 'You know he's almost a parallel to Peter – they both lose…I lose a father. He loses a father figure – his uncle. And then, especially in this third one, he's avenging his uncle's death, and I'm doing the same – I'm avenging my father's death. They've given me a lot. And the great thing about the character too is that he develops through all three films. His arc is not completed until this last film and in every movie he's different. It's the same path, but it's further along in the development, and it makes doing another movie more interesting.'

HAVOK (ALEX SUMMERS)

⚜ Appears in: *X-Men: First Class* (2011)

⚜ Powers: Ability to absorb solar energy

⚜ First comic-book appearance: March 1969

Havok is a mutant who struggles to control his ability to shoot red beams from his body. He is a likeable character and was played by Lucas Till in *X-Men: First Class.*

The film's producer Bryan Singer told the *Los Angeles Times*: 'I really, really like Havok, who we're bringing in at a sort of a different time, relative to the comic-book lore. It's an extremely cool character. What's great, too, about all of these characters is that they haven't honed their abilities yet. Havok is a danger to himself and everyone around him. That's where this movie is at – the recruiting of these mutants and bringing them together.'

In the comics, Havok is the younger brother of Cyclops but this wasn't the case in the movie. Bryan confessed: 'Yes, the time line is different...It wouldn't physically fit for him to be the brother of Cyclops. We take some liberties on that. There are notions, but, um, I don't want to give away certain interrelations, but let's just say there are some things that do adhere to the comics and do so in a way the fans will get a kick out of. And those things can, perhaps, move forward into the future...That's one reason we wanted to call the film *First Class* even though it isn't the *First Class* in the comics as fans know it. You couldn't really tell that story without going even earlier and explaining how they got there and how it came to be. I liked the title, so we kept it, but this is a prelude in a way that will eventually lead to the [story arcs and scenarios] that fit in more clearly with the *First Class* comics and situations.'

DID YOU KNOW?

Lucas Till played the love interest in Taylor Swift's music video for 'You Belong with Me'.

HAWKEYE (CLINT BARTON)

Appears in: *The Avengers* (2012)

Powers: Superb archer and fighter, with acrobatic skills

First comic-book appearance: September 1964

Clint is an amazing archer and can hit targets that would seem impossible to anyone else. He also excels at acrobatics and knife throwing – skills he picked up from growing up in a circus, the Carson Carnival of Travelling Wonder. He was trained by criminals, and one of them, the Swordsman, tried to kill him when Clint discovered that he was stealing from the circus. His parents are both dead after his dad drove when drunk and he has one brother called Barney who is loyal to the Swordsman despite what he tried to do to Clint.

Clint decides to be a superhero and his trying to help the innocent when he witnesses Iron Man in action. He goes on to date Black Widow, a fellow member of the Avengers.

Hawkeye traditionally wears a purple outfit but this was changed for *The Avengers* film. They decided to have him wear something that looked like a uniform rather than a superhero costume. The actor chosen to play Clint and Hawkeye was Jeremy Renner. Jeremy has been nominated for two Oscars so far, once for his performance in the 2008 film *The Hurt Locker* and then again in 2010 for his role in *The Town*. Having received these nominations really impressed the people who were casting *The Avengers* and looking for an actor to play Hawkeye.

Marvel Studio's Kevin Feige told a reporter from IGN: 'We hope to develop a standalone franchise for him [Jeremy] after *The Avengers*…

'Another reason why you go for an actor like Renner is you hope not to just cast an ensemble. It's an ensemble that you

hope are rich enough and real enough and the actor can portray and embody this enough that they can crack out and carry their own film.'

No doubt Jeremy would love to have his own Hawkeye movie one day.

HELLBOY

 Appears in: *Hellboy* (2004) and *Hellboy II: The Golden Army* (2008)

Powers: Super-strength, slow to age, can survive being shot and stabbed thanks to his ability to heal

First comic-book appearance: 1993

Hellboy is a demon with super-strength and a stone right hand. He works for the B.P.R.D., which stands for the Bureau for Paranormal Research and Defence. He is played by Ron Perlman in both films, although Montse Ribé plays him in the first flashback. Ron had to spend hours getting made up – it took the make-up artists and costume people up to six hours some days to turn him into Hellboy. Ron didn't mind too much and just saw it as part of the job. He actually thought the intense make-up and costume routine helped him get into character as he started to walk like Hellboy once it was on. He literally became a real-life Hellboy.

In the first film we get to see how Hellboy arrived on Earth. The evil Grigori Rasputin and some Nazi soldiers have opened a portal in the hope that they can free the Ogdru Jahad. They are the Dragons of Revelation and Rasputin believes they will destroy the world and form a new paradise. The Allies send in a team to stop this happening and they succeed in destroying the portal, although two key Nazis escape; Rasputin is swallowed up

by the portal and a demon baby makes it through… they call him Hellboy. He is adopted by Trevor Broom who brings him up as though he's human.

He grows up and gets a job working for the B.P.R.D. alongside Liz Sherman, Abe Sapien and John Myers. Sixty years may have passed since Rasputin disappeared through the portal, but when his Nazi friends decide it's time to bring him back, the B.P.R.D. have to see that they put an end to him once and for all. Rasputin, Kroenen and Haupstein unleash a monster called Sammael who is given the power of reincarnation. Each time he is killed he multiplies, which makes him one tough opponent. Liz unintentionally knocks herself, Hellboy and John out for the count when she uses her powers, and Rasputin seizes them. He tries to convince Hellboy to become the Ogdru Jahad (his real identity) by threatening to harm Liz. Hellboy decides to do it but John manages to talk him out of it by telling him he can control his own destiny. Hellboy rips off his Ogdru Jahad horns and stabs Rasputin. Rasputin's body opens to reveal the monster Behemoth. Hellboy comes up with a plan. He lets the huge Behemoth swallow him but sets off hand grenades, which kills the monster.

His actions save Liz's life and they kiss.

In the second film, Hellboy and his friends go up against a magical creature called Prince Nuada who is searching for three pieces of a crown to give him ultimate power over the Golden Army. He hates humans and wants to destroy them. He doesn't care who he kills to get the pieces, even killing his own father to get his hands on the second piece. His sister goes on the run with the third and final piece.

On a personal level, things aren't going well for Hellboy who is struggling living with Liz and hates the fact that the B.P.R.D. are a secret agency. He ends up having his identity blown, something that doesn't go down well with his superiors. He is demoted and Johann Krauss is brought in to lead the team. Abe Sapien finds out that Liz is pregnant but Hellboy doesn't know.

The team step in to protect Nuada's sister, Nuala – and Abe falls in love with her. Hellboy defeats a forest god and troll who attacked Nuala on behalf of her brother. Nuada arrives at the headquarters and manages to kidnap his sister and mortally wounds Hellboy. His friends take him to the Angel of Death who saves him after Liz begs him to. She tells Hellboy he is going to be a dad, which gives him something to fight for.

Abe hands over the final piece of the crown to save Nuala, which allows Nuada control over the Golden Army. Hellboy challenges him to a battle and Nuada has to accept because he is a member of Hell's royalty. They fight and when it looks like Hellboy could be defeated Nuala kills herself, which in turn causes Nuada to feel her pain as they share a special bond. They both die and turn to stone.

Liz destroys the crown, which means that the Golden Army will never be awakened again. Hellboy and his team decide to leave the B.P.R.D. but will fight again. Liz lets slip that she is expecting twins.

THE HULK (BRUCE BANNER)

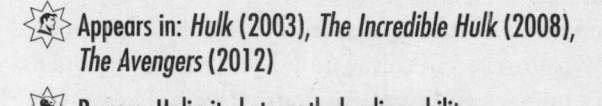

Appears in: *Hulk* (2003), *The Incredible Hulk* (2008), *The Avengers* (2012)

Powers: Unlimited strength, healing ability

First comic-book appearance: May 1962

The actor chosen to play Bruce and the Hulk in the 2003 film was Eric Bana. Edward Norton was also in the running to play the lead but didn't like the script – he went on to play Bruce and the Hulk in the 2008 film.

In the first film, Hulk's history is explored; we learn that Bruce's dad David spent a long time in a mental institution after

causing an explosion which killed his wife – he had wanted to kill Bruce because he was scared of what his mutation could turn him into.

In the present day, Bruce is also interested in genetics (like his dad) and works alongside the Army General's daughter Betty Ross as a researcher in a lab. Glenn Talbot wants them to work for him but they refuse.

His dad David is released from the institution and tries to get as close to him as possible, even getting a caretaker's job in the same building. He wants to know about Bruce's mutations.

Bruce ends up getting involved in an experiment that causes radiation to combine with his abnormal DNA – turning him into the Hulk. He ends up being arrested by the military when he is forced to save Betty from three mutant dogs (who have been created and released by his dad). Betty wants her dad to help Bruce but General Ross is more concerned with the danger Hulk poses.

Glenn Talbot makes a big mistake when he takes matters into his own hands in an attempt to gain a DNA sample and ends up causing Bruce to transform into the Hulk again and escape the military base. He comes under attack from tanks and helicopters as he goes in search of Betty. She convinces her dad to let her talk to Bruce and he reluctantly agrees. David is hungry for power and asks Bruce to let him absorb his Hulk powers but he refuses. Bruce ends up turning into the Hulk as his dad bites into an electrical wire and transforms himself before attacking him. During their battle David keeps changing appearance as they fight in the sky, on the ground and by the lake. In the end the Hulk agrees to share his power, which has fatal results for David. He turns into an energy bubble and explodes when General Ross uses a Gamma charge bomb. Bruce manages to survive because he is underwater at the time.

The final scene of the film shows Bruce secretly working in the Amazon rainforest and warning thieves to not take his

vital medical supplies. He tells them, 'You won't like it when I'm angry.'

The 2003 film wasn't a big hit with cinema audiences but people still loved the character of the Hulk so a second film was made. This film had a new cast and was a reboot. It started five years after Bruce had gone on the run.

Bruce has been keeping his head down working in a soda factory in Rio de Janeiro. He hopes he can find a cure for his condition one day so that he doesn't turn into the Hulk every time he becomes angry. He keeps a note of the number of days he has gone without transforming – knowing that he will have to move location if he does so that the US military can't track him down. He is researching possible herbal-based cures with the help of an expert he has met on the Internet – who he calls Mr Blue. Both men are keeping their names and locations a secret. Bruce has also been looking at how meditation could help him control the Hulk side of himself by slowing down his breathing.

Bruce is popular with his boss at the factory and has settled in the town but soon has to move again when he cuts his finger and a drop of his unique blood ends up in a soda bottle which is shipped to the USA. The person who drinks it dies and General Ross is able to track where the bottle came from. He arrives at the factory alongside Emil Blonsky and his men.

After Bruce transforms and escapes, General Ross comes up with a new plan. He has Blonsky injected with a special serum that makes him more agile, faster, improves his stamina and allows him to heal quicker. He becomes a super soldier!

Bruce decides to return to Culver University in Virginia where Betty still works. She has moved on in the last five years and is now dating a psychiatrist called Leonard Samson, but it is clear that she still has feelings for Bruce. Although Betty is loyal to Bruce, Leonard isn't, and he lets General Ross know that Bruce is in the area. He soon arrives with Blonsky and Bruce is forced to turn

into the Hulk. He fights with Blonsky and manages to defeat him. The Hulk saves Betty's life during the fight and leaves with her.

Bruce and Betty go on the run and Bruce contacts the one man he thinks can help him – Mr Blue. He explains the situation and Mr Blue (Dr Samuel Sterns) tells him to come to New York. Once they meet he reveals that he might have a cure but ideally he would have liked more time. They do a small test but still don't know whether the cure will be permanent. Samuel has been blending Bruce's blood samples so that he has a lab full. It turns out that he wants to use the blood he has 'produced' on humans to give them some of the Hulk's powers. Bruce is horrified because he knows the damage that could be caused if the wrong people end up 'superhuman'. He tries to convince Samuel that it is a bad idea but the professor won't listen. General Ross arrives and both Bruce and Betty are arrested. Blonsky might have been turned into a super soldier but he still wants more power and forces Samuel to inject him with a cocktail of Bruce's blood and other chemicals. Samuel warns him how dangerous it is because of the super soldier serum he already has in his system – he thinks Blonsky could turn into an 'Abomination'.

The new monster created is stronger and more powerful than the Hulk and Blonsky is able to control him mentally. Bruce has never been able to do this with the Hulk. The Abomination runs around the city destroying things and causing mayhem – desperate for the Hulk to come and fight him. Bruce is in a helicopter at this point, under the military's control, but asks General Ross to let him go so he can fight. Betty is very worried but Bruce insists it's something he has to do. He jumps from the helicopter, turning into the Hulk as he falls.

Hulk and the Abomination fight ferociously and the battle only ends when the Hulk manages to wrap a huge metal chain around the Abomination, almost strangling him to death. He only backs off when Betty tells him to.

The next we see of Bruce he is in Bella Coola and instead of trying not to transform at all, he is learning to control the Hulk. In another scene Tony Stark discusses with General Ross that he is putting a team together (The Avengers).

DID YOU KNOW?

Lou Ferrigno, who played the Hulk in the TV series, actually voiced the Hulk in this movie.

Edward Norton fully expected to play Bruce and the Hulk in *The Avengers* film but ended up getting replaced by his friend Mark Ruffalo. Back in July 2010 Kevin Feige, the president of Marvel, released a statement. In it he said: 'We have made the decision to not bring Ed Norton back to portray the role of Bruce Banner in *The Avengers*. Our decision is definitely not one based on monetary factors, but instead rooted in the need for an actor who embodies the creativity and collaborative spirit of our other talented cast members.

'*The Avengers* demands players who thrive working as part of an ensemble, as evidenced by Robert (Downey Jr), Chris H (Hemsworth), Chris E (Evans), Sam (L Jackson), Scarlett (Johansson), and all of our talented casts. We are looking to announce a name actor who fulfils these requirements and is passionate about the iconic role in the coming weeks.'

Edward was very upset when he found out what the statement said and his agent decided to release his own statement in response. In it he said: 'This offensive statement from Kevin Feige at Marvel is a purposefully misleading, inappropriate attempt to paint our client in a negative light.

'Here are the facts: two months ago, Kevin called me and said he wanted Edward to reprise the role of Bruce Banner in *The Avengers*. He told me it would be his fantasy to bring Edward on

stage with the rest of the cast at Comic-Con and make it the event of the convention. When I said that Edward was definitely open to this idea, Kevin was very excited and we agreed that Edward should meet with Joss Whedon to discuss the project. Edward and Joss had a very good meeting (confirmed by Feige to me) at which Edward said he was enthusiastic at the prospect of being a part of the ensemble cast.

'Marvel subsequently made him a financial offer to be in the film and both sides started negotiating in good faith. This past Wednesday, after several weeks of civil, uncontentious discussions, but before we had come to terms on a deal, a representative from Marvel called to say they had decided to go in another direction with the part. This seemed to us to be a financial decision but, whatever the case, it is completely their prerogative, and we accepted their decision with no hard feelings.'

It's such a shame that Edward won't be playing the Hulk again because he did such a great job. Even Mark Ruffalo felt a bit funny about how Edward was dropped and he got the part because they are mates. He realised how big the part is at Comic-Con, which is a huge comic-book convention held in San Diego each year that also promotes fantasy novels, video games and films. Mark had to stand alongside the other big names appearing in *The Avengers* film.

He said: 'It was very exciting – and I realised I had some pretty big shoes to fill. Those were my heroes up there! I was a comic-book fan growing up. I loved the Hulk and the Avengers – it's just strange to be entering that world as an actor. I never would have imagined that before.'

He talked to the journalists there about how he sees Bruce. 'He's a guy struggling with two sides of himself – the dark and the light – and everything he does in his life is filtered through issues of control,' he revealed. 'I grew up on the Bill Bixby TV series, which I thought was a really nuanced and real human way to look at the Hulk. I like that the part has those qualities.'

In one interview Mark said that he would be playing the Hulk as well as Bruce, as he won't be CGI-generated like he had been in other films. This was contradicted by stunt man Brandon Molale on 27 January 2011 when he tweeted: 'My life: Just auditioned to play the Hulk (motion capture) in the new Avengers film. Pretty damn cool job!'

We will just have to wait and see whether Mark, Brandon or another actor gets the job – or whether CGI will be used after all.

HUMAN TORCH (JOHNNY STORM)

Appears in: *Fantastic Four* (2005), *Fantastic Four: Rise of the Silver Surfer* (2007)

Powers: Can cover his body with flames, control fire and fly

First comic-book appearance: November 1961

Johnny Storm is a cocky astronaut who used to work for NASA but now works for Victor von Doom. He might mess around a lot but he's not stupid; in fact he is highly intelligent. He goes on a mission into space with his boss, fellow astronaut Ben Grimm, his sister Susan and scientist Reed Richards. The mission almost ends in disaster when they come into contact with a cosmic cloud but they don't die – they just end up with special powers.

Johnny gains the ability to engulf himself in flames and fly – taking the nickname the Human Torch. He loves the fame and celebrity status that comes with being a member of the Fantastic Four.

In the first film he uses his brains to evade a heat-seeking missile sent by Doctor Doom and then helps defeat him; in the second film he is the one who saves the day again when he manages to dislodge Doctor Doom from the Silver

Surfer's board by taking on the powers of the other Fantastic Four members.

The actor who played Johnny Storm and the Human Torch in both films was Chris Evans who is actually quite the opposite of Johnny as he is a humble guy who never lets fame get to his head. He loved playing Johnny and told journalist Rob Alicea: 'It was fun. He's more energy than anything else. He loves life. I think that his arrogance is a by-product of that energy.'

Playing Johnny was tiring and all the actors on set felt under pressure because the studio had decided the exact date the first film would be released — before filming even started. This is an unusual approach, especially considering the special effects that would be in the film. Chris found the long hours on set each day a challenge: 'It took a lot of juice every day…Your energy level just starts to take a nosedive around noon everyday.

'You come to work every day playing this guy and you still have all this energy to crack jokes; you can't help but take that home with you.'

As well as having to learn his lines to prepare to play Johnny, Chris had to work out a lot. He has always gone the gym with his mates, so he just put in more sessions and he already had a good diet so he didn't need to change that.

DID YOU KNOW?

Chris is a huge *Star Wars* fan and loves watching the old movies whenever he can.

I IS FOR...

ICEMAN (BOBBY DRAKE)

- Appears in: *X-Men* (2000), *X2* (2003), *X-Men: The Last Stand* (2006)
- Powers: Ability to change the temperature and freeze himself and others
- First comic-book appearance: September 1963

Bobby can turn his whole body to ice and anything around him. He became a good friend of Rogue when she came to the school and they started to date. They avoid kissing to start with because she would hurt him – she can absorb someone's powers just by touching them – but one day Bobby decides to take the plunge. They kiss and in the beginning it seems like things are okay, but eventually Bobby has to pull away, for his own safety.

Bobby's biggest rival is Pyro. Bobby also hangs around with Kitty Pryde, which makes Rogue jealous. She doesn't want to lose Bobby so seeks a cure. She's willing to lose her mutant powers if it means she can be physically close to Bobby.

Bobby's brother is jealous of his powers and actually reports him to the police when he visits home. Wolverine ends up getting shot because of Bobby's brother's actions but thankfully suffers no long-term damage.

The actor who played Bobby and Iceman in the *X-Men* films was Shawn Ashmore. Some people mistakenly think that the guy who played Jimmy in *Smallville* played him but that is wrong. They are twins: Aaron Ashmore is in *Smallville* and Shawn Ashmore is in the *X-Men* films!

DID YOU KNOW?

Both Shawn and Aaron have a tattoo on their wrists that says GMA (Good Man Ashmore). Shawn has it on his right wrist and Aaron has it on his left.

INVISIBLE WOMAN (SUE STORM)

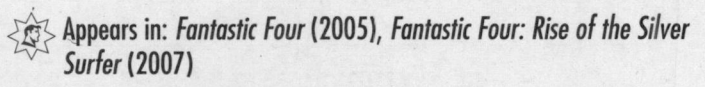 Appears in: *Fantastic Four* (2005), *Fantastic Four: Rise of the Silver Surfer* (2007)

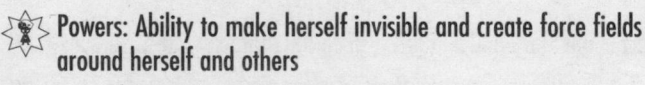 Powers: Ability to make herself invisible and create force fields around herself and others

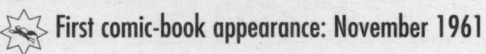 First comic-book appearance: November 1961

Sue is a scientist and researcher. She was dating Victor von Doom before the cosmic cloud incident but turned him down when he proposed. After she gained her invisibility powers she became

closer to Reed Richards (Mr Fantastic). Her powers are influenced by her feelings. Reed proposed and she knew then that he was the man she wanted to marry. Their first wedding day ended in disaster when the Silver Surfer turned up.

The Silver Surfer was fond of Sue and ended up using his powers to bring her back to life after Doctor Doom stabbed her. She reminded him of a girl he used to be in love with himself, and it is because of Sue and the kindness she showed him that he decided to rebel against his MASTER Galactus.

The actress Jessica Alba played Sue Storm in both films. She met her husband Cash Warren on the set of *Fantastic Four* as he was the director's assistant. She actually thinks she shares quite a few of Sue's qualities – she can be overemotional and controlling at times.

In an interview with Radio Free Entertainment it was clear that Jessica loves Sue. She said: 'Sue Storm is a positive role model because she doesn't do anything manipulative or destructive. She really is trying to do the right thing, and really is trying to keep this family unit together, and I think that's great. There aren't enough young women that are being portrayed in that way. And the movie itself is about people finding solutions to their problems versus just breaking apart and running away from them. And once you unite as a family, then can you save the world. It's so epic…but it's a lovely message.'

DID YOU KNOW?

The director Tim Story had a huge crush on the character Sue Storm when he was a little boy.

Before filming started each member of the Fantastic Four had to have a body cast done so that the costumes were precisely the right size. That meant they had to strip off until they were

wearing just their underwear and then they were covered in Vaseline. This wasn't at all glamorous and it made Jessica feel a bit self-conscious because strangers helped her apply it everywhere. It was worth it, though, because the outfits fitted perfectly.

Once filming started Jessica had to be helped into her spandex Fantastic Four suit each day by several costume assistants. They had to use a special tool to make sure the suit was worn correctly – and the costume had zips on the inside, which could pinch.

IRON MAN (TONY STARK)

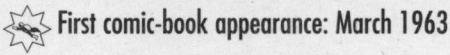 Appears in: *Iron Man* (2008), *The Incredible Hulk* (2008), *Iron Man 2* (2010), *The Avengers* (2012)

 Powers: His arc reactor suit has advanced weaponry including a machine gun; it also allows him to fly and gives him the ability to fire repulsor beams, super-strength and durability

First comic-book appearance: March 1963

Tony Stark is a billionaire weapons manufacturer who takes on the identity of Iron Man after he is kidnapped in Afghanistan. In order to escape from the terrorist group that is holding him he builds a suit that enables him to defeat dozens of men and blast himself to safety. Tony has always been a playboy and a cocky kind of guy but his priorities change once he returns to his normal life. He knows that the men who held him captive were using guns that his company (Stark Industries) made. This results in him announcing that Stark Industries will no longer be making weapons.

Stark Industries executive Obadiah Stane isn't at all pleased and tells Tony that he is risking the future of Stark Industries and tarnishing his father's memory. Tony just shrugs his concerns aside and carries on doing what he wants.

Tony has always been an inventor like his father and sets about creating another suit. He also improves a temporary arc reactor and electromagnet fitted to his chest that was created whilst he was imprisoned. He needs to wear it to stop shrapnel entering his heart.

Tony discovers that Stane is trying to take over Stark Industries, which infuriates him. When he finds out that the terrorists that captured him are using his weapons to destroy the village of the man who helped him escape he heads there straight away — in his new suit. He soon defeats them to the delight of the villagers who thought they were doomed. As he attempts to fly out of the country he is deemed a risk by the US military who are controlling the skies. They don't know what he is and decide to attack him using two F-22 Raptor jets. He ends up calling his friend Lieutenant Colonel James Rhodes who has the power to stop the attack, but he escapes anyway without needing his friend's help.

Tony asks his personal assistant (and loyal friend) Pepper Potts to help him discover the truth about Stane and sends her into the headquarters to hack into the computer system. He wants to know what Stane has been doing behind his back. Pepper finds files proving that Stane had arranged for Tony to be killed by the terrorists in Afghanistan but that it was the terrorists who had decided to hold him ransom instead because they realised how much money their captive was worth. Their weapons had been supplied by Stane, too. Pepper almost gets caught by Stane when he catches her in the office but she cleverly uses a newspaper to cover the pen drive she has stuck in the computer in order to copy the damning files. She leaves quickly but is scared he is going to follow her. In the foyer she bumps into Agent Coulson from the S.H.I.E.L.D. counterterrorism agency who had been waiting to speak to her. They go somewhere private and she explains what Stane has been up to.

Meanwhile, Stane has visited the original terrorists and

retrieved what remains of Tony's first suit. It had fallen to pieces soon after he escaped. Stane kills them and then takes the suit to his own team of scientists. He wants a suit better than Iron Man's, one that will give him ultimate power. The scientists do their best but they can't produce an arc reactor like Tony has. Stane won't give up and breaks into Tony's home. He immobilises him by using a sonic device that prevents Tony from moving or speaking but at the same time allows him to watch exactly what is happening. Stane rips the arc reactor and leaves Tony to die.

Pepper, Agent Coulson and his colleagues arrive at Stark Industries to arrest Stane but they are shocked to find him in a humongous metal suit. Pepper runs for her life as Stane easily disposes of the agents.

Back at Tony's home James (Colonel Rhodes) arrives and finds his friend close to death. He manages to help him insert his first arc reactor and put on his suit before he leaves in his car. Tony blasts through the roof and flies as fast as he can to Stane and Pepper's location. Once there he fights Stane, but he isn't as strong as he normally is because of the arc reactor he is using. Stane is much stronger. Tony manages to draw Stane onto the roof so that Pepper can overload the full-sized arc reactor. The electrical surge that is generated knocks Stane out and sends him through the roof. He lands on the arc reactor and it kills him. Pepper thinks that Tony might be dead too because of what she has done but he managed to survive because he rolled over at just the right time.

The next day a press conference is held. Agent Coulson has given Tony an alibi but Tony can't resist revealing to the press that he is the 'Iron Man' they are all talking about. He laps up the attention before leaving the stage. Later, Tony is visited by S.H.I.E.L.D. director Nick Fury who announces that Iron Man isn't the only superhero in the world and that he wants to discuss the Avenger Initiative. S.H.I.E.L.D. stands for the Strategic Homeland Intervention, Enforcement and Logistics Division.

In *Iron Man II*, Tony has revealed to the world that he is Iron Man. A man called Ivan Vanko who is grieving for his dad, sees Tony, on TV. He is a Russian physicist and hates Tony because Tony's dad betrayed his own dad, Anton Vanko. Anton gave up everything to go and work with Tony's dad only to get fired and send back to the Soviet Union. Ivan wants revenge.

Tony has been using his Iron Man suit to help uphold world peace. The general public might love Iron Man but the US government are less keen and demand Tony hands over his suit and the Iron Man technology to them. He promptly refuses. He doesn't see why he should hand over something that he created and which belongs to him.

Tony might appear confident on the outside but on the inside he is desperately worried. The core of his arc reactor is made from a chemical element called palladium and it is slowly poisoning him. He has tried to find an alternative but nothing else works. He knows it is going to kill him but he won't say anything to Pepper or his friends. He decides instead to just try and enjoy the time he has left – and take as many risks as possible.

He wants Pepper to have control of Stark Industries when he dies, so appoints her CEO. He gets another assistant called Natalie Rushman to be her replacement. Whilst Tony is enjoying being in Monte Carlo for the Grand Prix he decides to race himself – to Pepper's horror. During the race Ivan Vanko appears, destroying cars with his whip-like weapon that is powered by his arc reactor suit. He attacks Tony's car and if it hadn't been for Pepper and Happy's quick thinking, Tony would have been a goner. They drive on to the track, try to run down Ivan and throw Tony the case that transforms into his Iron Man suit. Tony manages to defeat him and Ivan is sent to prison.

Tony discovers why Ivan wants him dead, and that his dad had had to extradite Anton Vanko because he wanted to profit from the first arc reactor they built. He lived the rest of his life in

poverty before dying, which is why Ivan has a grudge against the Stark family.

Tony's rival Justin Hammer figures that if Tony won't hand over his suit to the US government so he can copy it, then he will ask Ivan to help him build one. He helps Ivan escape from prison by faking his death, stupidly thinking that he can outsmart him. He gets Ivan to build military drones using the suit that James provided to the military. James was so disgusted by Tony's behaviour at his birthday party that he put on the spare Mark II suit, fought him and then left with the suit. James didn't know that Tony thought it would be his last birthday party before he died.

He re-establishes his dad's Stark Expo, which is an international technology exhibition. Its slogan is 'Better living through technology'. It will be the first Stark Expo since 1974.

DID YOU KNOW?

If you type 'Stark Expo' into Google then you can visit a site that has been set up to look like the official Stark Expo website. You can read a letter from Tony, watch videos and see a virtual drawing of what it would look like.

Tony decides to reinstate the Stark Expo after Nick Fury visits him with Natalie, only she is revealed to be an undercover agent called Natasha Romanoff. Nick explains to Tony that his dad Howard was one of S.H.I.E.L.D.'s founders and helps him find a hidden message in the model of the 1974 Stark Expo – a diagram of the structure of a new element which could potentially save his life. He goes ahead and uses the new element on his own arc reactor after receiving a message from Ivan telling him he is alive and wants revenge. The new element works well and Tony can abandon using palladium from then on.

Meanwhile, Justin decides to unveil his drones at the Stark Expo to take the attention away from Tony. Ivan has other ideas. After the drones and James in the War Hammer suit are revealed, he commands them to attack Tony/Iron Man. James is powerless to stop as Ivan has complete control of his suit. Iron Man quickly flies outside and attempts to escape the drones. Justin gets arrested and Natatalie/Natasha heads to Justin's headquarters with Happy to try and apprehend Ivan. He manages to escape, but the duo manage to give James control over his War Hammer suit again.

Once James's suit comes under his control again he rushes to the side of Iron Man and they fight together to defeat the remaining drones and Ivan. They might not be able to defeat Ivan individually but together they can by firing repulsor rays at them. Ivan's suit becomes damaged and without it he is virtually powerless. Once he realises that it is all over for him Ivan activates the self-destruct device, which blows up himself and the drones. The blast destroys the Stark Expo complex but Iron Man and War Machine survive. Iron Man saves Pepper and they kiss, with her resigning as CEO of Stark Industries.

Later, Nick Fury tells Tony that Iron Man is a suitable candidate for the Avengers Initiative and he agrees to be a consultant. He insists that he and James receive bravery medals from Senator Stern – knowing that Stern will hate every minute, having objected to Tony keeping his suit.

Robert Downey Jr plays Tony Stark and Iron Man. Robert really wanted to work with Jon Favreau the director of both *Iron Man* films, and this is one of the main reasons he agreed to play Tony/Iron Man. Robert actually helped write the script and made Tony more real. He didn't want Tony to turn into a goody two-shoes the second he became Iron Man; he wanted to keep the cheeky, humorous qualities his character showed early on in the film.

DID YOU KNOW?

The director Jon Favreau actually appears in the movies as Happy Hogan, Tony's bodyguard and chauffeur.

To get himself fit before shooting started, Robert did weight training five days a week and some martial arts training. He had to look good but also needed to build up his stamina for the long days he would spend shooting the action scenes.

Iron Man 3 will hit cinemas in 2013 and will not be directed by Jon Favreau. It is not known if Jon will still appear as Happy Hogan. Shane Black is the director tipped for the job but Robert will be helping direct too, according to reports.

J IS FOR...

JEAN GREY (PHOENIX)

- Appears in: *X-Men* (2000), *X2* (2003), *X-Men: The Last Stand* (2006)
- Powers: Telepathy, can move objects with her mind, and when she is the Phoenix has unimaginable powers
- First comic-book appearance: September 1963

Jean is doctor for the X-Men and is dating Scott (Cyclops) although she is close to Wolverine, too. She is only capable of moving small objects with her telekinetic powers but manages to do more in certain situations. In the first film she stopped Toad mid-jump and supported Wolverine as he travelled via wind to the top of the Statue of Liberty. She also uses Professor X's Cerebro machine but in doing so puts herself at risk. The

Cerebro is a device that is used to detect where mutants and humans are located. When Rogue runs away, Professor X is able to find out where she is by using the Cerebro. Jean uses it to find Magneto but it overpowers her and she can't control it.

It is thought that either the Cerebro or Magneto's machine caused her to become the Phoenix.

In the second film Jean is experiencing stronger telekinetic powers and she is worried about dreams she has been having. She is showing more signs of being the Phoenix; her eyes glow red and her body also glows red as she fights Cyclops – under the control of William Stryker. She manages to repair the X-Jet telekinetically, stop Nightcrawler's teleportation and uses Professor X to send Cyclops a message. At Alkali Lake she has the strength to hold back a huge amount of water, which goes on to create a tidal wave. Once everyone is safe she releases the water and it engulfs her.

In *X-Men: The Last Stand* Jean might have gone but Cyclops is constantly getting telepathic messages from her. He returns to the lake where she died and unleashes his optic blasts on the lake. This cause Jean to appear from the water and they embrace. As they kiss, Jean removes Cyclops' visor and she controls his optic blasts. She can do it but he has never been able to fully control them himself – this shows how powerful she has become. The kiss turns into the kiss of death as Cyclops' face distorts. Professor X senses that Cyclops is dead and sends Wolverine and Storm to the lake. They find no sign of their friend apart from his visor and discover Jean unconscious.

It turns out that Jean's weakened powers in the past had been caused by restrictions placed on her by Professor X. He had realised when she was younger that she had unimaginable powers and had put psychic barriers around her subconscious to control them. This had actually caused her to develop two personalities – Jean and the Phoenix. She turned into the Phoenix when she couldn't control her powers – which is extremely dangerous.

When she held back the water and sacrificed herself she became the Phoenix.

Once Wolverine and Storm return with Jean, Professor X explains what he did and then leaves Wolverine alone with her. She wakes up and kisses Wolverine and it seems like the old Jean is back, but then she changes; she becomes overly aggressive and has a breakdown. Wolverine is stunned and tries to talk to her about Professor X and Cyclops but this makes things worse and her Phoenix side emerges. She renders him unconscious before escaping and heads for the house she grew up in, where she is soon joined by Professor X and Magneto. They each want her: Professor X wants to help her and Magneto wants her for himself and his evil plans. Jean is extremely disorientated and when Professor X mentions Cyclops' death she turns into the Phoenix. They use telepathy to fight each other and Phoenix causes objects around them to disintegrate and gravity to flip. She changes appearance too: her eyes turn black, her veins become visible under her skin and her hair changes to a fiery red colour. She no longer cares about Professor X and lifts him up out of his chair along with the whole house. She doesn't want him in her head any more. His last words to her are, 'Don't let it control you.' Wolverine witnesses Professor X's final moments before he breaks up into small particles and the house crashes to the ground. Phoenix leaves with Magneto.

Later, during the attack on the labs producing the mutant cure, Phoenix looks unstoppable, destroying people, mutants and buildings with her maximised power. She is letting her power control her. Only Wolverine can stand against her because every time she tries to cause him to disintegrate, his body heals him. He begs Jean the Phoenix to stop, but she won't. Then the Jean part of her surfaces and asks him to stop the Phoenix. Wolverine declares his love for her and then stabs her. She is later buried alongside Cyclops and Professor X.

The actress chosen to play Jean Grey (the Phoenix) was

Famke Janssen. When a young version of Jean is shown being taught by Professor X in *X-Men: The Last Stand* it was teen actress Haley Ramm who portrayed her.

JOHANN KRAUS

Appears in: *Hellboy II: The Golden Army* (2008)

Powers: Can be overtaken by spirits, which can be useful in certain situations

First comic-book appearance: 2003

Johann Kraus is a B.P.R.D. agent who is sent in to run the team once Hellboy's identity is revealed. He is a German psychic who wears a special suit, which keeps him alive. He is a disembodied ectoplasmic spirit, so needs the containment suit. He is alive but he doesn't have a body since it was destroyed by a shock wave during a séance (according to the *Hellboy* comics). In the film no clear explanation is given apart from that it involved a woman he loved and whose ring he carries with him.

He went to the B.P.R.D. for help and they put him in a special tank before they created his containment suit. It was designed by Trevor Bruttenholm.

Two actors shared the part of Johann – John Alexander and James Dodd. Another actor called Seth MacFarlane provided his voice. The suit was extremely heavy as the actor had to wear a helmet made from glass and mirrors helping to disguise his head.

JUBILEE (JUBILATION LEE)

Appears in: *X-Men* (2000), *X2* (2003), *X-Men: The Last Stand* (2006)

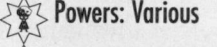 Powers: Generates and fires energy globules

First comic-book appearance: May 1989

Jubilee is a mutant with the ability to generate energy globules from her fingertips. She is able to control where her 'fireworks' end up by using her mind. She is a student at Professor X's school and was kidnapped alongside five other students when the X-Mansion was invaded by Stryker. Nightcrawler and Storm rescued them and brought them home.

She was played by Katrina Florece in *X-Men* and Kea Wong in *X2* and *X-Men: The Last Stand*.

JUSTICE LEAGUE

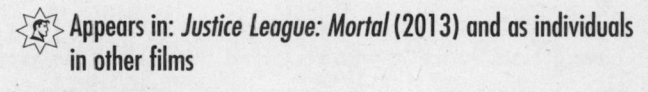 Appears in: *Justice League: Mortal* (2013) and as individuals in other films

Powers: Various

First comic-book appearance: February 1960

The Justice League of America is a team of superheroes who protect Earth and its people. The official members of the Justice League are Superman, Batman, Martian Manhunter, Aquaman, Wonderwoman, Flash and Green Lantern.

They have fought against a whole host of enemies, including the Manhunter robots from the planet Oa, Johnny Sorrow, Despero and Mageddon.

A *Justice League of America* film is in the pipeline, but Warner Bros will need to find new actors to play the big roles first. Ryan Reynolds is expected to play Green Lantern.

K IS FOR...

KATO

Appears in: *The Green Hornet* (2011)

Powers: Martial arts expert

First comic-book appearance: December 1940

Before Britt Reid's (The Green Hornet) dad died Kato was just a chauffeur who made amazing coffee whenever he was asked to. After the funeral, Britt fires his dad's staff only to find that his coffee tastes awful. He quickly asks Kato back and starts to learn more about the man who has been making him coffee for years.

Kato is the real superhero of the Green Hornet movie as he is a martial arts expert. He might be Green Hornet's sidekick but he is the one who defeats the most bad guys. Britt isn't a born

fighter and gets himself into trouble all the time. Kato is the brains of the duo and he created their Black Beauty car.

The actor chosen to play Kato in the movie was Jay Chou.

DID YOU KNOW?

Jay is a huge pop and R&B singer in Asia and has won four World Music Awards!

KAYLA SILVERFOX

- Appears in: *X-Men Origins: Wolverine* (2009)
- Powers: Tactile hypnosis (she can control what people think and do as long as she has physical contact with them)
- First comic-book appearance: August 1989

Kayla is a mutant whose special ability is that she can control the mind of anyone she comes into contact with through touch. She dated Logan, before pretending to have been murdered by Victor (Logan's Brother) in order to have her sister released by William Stryker. She hated betraying Logan but she had no choice. She is devastated when Stryker won't do he promised and release her sister.

Logan chooses his alias Wolverine because of a story that Kayla told him about a spirit called Wolverine who was tricked into being parted from his lover, the moon, forever. He can look at her from afar but will never be close to her again.

Her sister Emma is a mutant who can harden her skin to be like diamonds, allowing her to act as a shield and prevent bullets making an impact. She also goes by the name White Queen. As they try to escape with the other mutant captives, Kayla is shot

but saves Wolverine's life. After Stryker shoots Wolverine in the head with adamantium bullets she controls Stryker's mind and tells him to drop the gun and keep walking. She then dies but Wolverine survives as his body heals itself, but his memory has been damaged and he doesn't recognise Kayla when he sees her dead body.

The actress chosen to play Kayla was American actress Lynn Collins.

KESTREL (JOHN WRAITH)

Appears in: *X-Men Origins: Wolverine* (2009)

Powers: Ability to teleport

First comic-book appearance: November 1991

Kestrel/John is a former member of Team X who becomes a boxing manager and coach when he leaves the team. His special ability is that he can teleport. He is the only former member of Team X that Logan fully trusts and he is the one he turns to when he wants to find out where William Stryker is. John advises Logan to speak to Fred Dukes and then goes with him to talk to the only mutant who has ever escaped Remy LeBeau. John goes outside but Victor arrives and they fight. John knows that Victor is killing all the former members of Team X and that he's next. Victor predicts John's movements and manages to grab his spine whilst he is teleporting. He enjoys seeing John in pain before snapping his spine and letting John drop dead. He later gives Kestrel's teleporting abilities to Deadpool.

Rapper Will.i.am played Kestrel in the movie. He was interviewed by journalist Kam Williams about the role and asked if he modelled him on anybody. Will.i.am replied: 'I modelled him after my cousin, Earl. He used to be a very, very bad, bad

man. He's done some bad, bad things, but he's also a very approachable, likable, huggable kind of guy. He has some bad friends who've done bad things, too, but he has a conscience.'

He went on to talk about Kestrel's relationship with Wolverine: 'He and Wolverine are close buddies. They go off into the world, and mess up things, but he has a heart, and knows when enough is enough.'

L IS FOR...

LEECH (JIMMY)

- Appears in: *X-Men: The Last Stand* (2006)
- Powers: Ability to temporarily remove the powers of mutants who come into contact with him
- First comic-book appearance: March 1984

Leech is a mutant who is unique in that he cancels the mutations of any mutant he comes into contact with, until they move a safe distance away from him. Leech is used by the pharmaceutical company Worthington Labs to create their mutant cure. Because he is their source they can't afford to let anything happen to him and so they keep him locked up.

Magneto recognises how vital Leech is and after finding that he being held at Alcatraz Island he rallies his troops and plans an

ambush. He wants Leech dead and the labs to be destroyed. Juggernaut is tasked with getting Leech whilst the others fight the X-Men. Kitty Pryde tries to stop him but he is a tough opponent and as she passes through the walls he breaks them down behind her. She reaches Leech first but because he cancels out her phasing powers they can't escape.

Juggernaut busts his way in and runs straight at them. They move at just the right time and he ends up hitting his head so hard against the wall that he knocks himself out. They are then able to use the holes that Juggernaut has left to quickly escape before any of Magneto's Brotherhood can stop them.

On leaving the Island Leech becomes a pupil at the school and can finally mix with other mutants instead of being confined to his own room.

The actor chosen to play Leech was Cameron Bright. Since playing Leech he has gone on to play Alec in the *Twilight Saga* films.

LIZ SHERMAN

Appears in: *Hellboy* (2004), *Hellboy II: The Golden Army* (2008)
Powers: Pyrokinetic abilities
First comic-book appearance: 1994

Liz Sherman is a human who has the power to control fire with her mind. She can control her powers most of the time, but when she first discovered she had them she couldn't. She ended up killing 32 people when she was 11, including her family.

The B.P.R.D. have taught her how to better control her abilities. She is dating Hellboy and at the end of *Hellboy II: The Golden Army* she reveals that she is expecting twins.

M IS FOR...

MOIRA MACTAGGERT

✦ Appears in: *X-Men: The Last Stand* (2006) and *X-Men: First Class* (2011)

✦ Powers: None

✦ First comic-book appearance: December 1975

Dr Moira MacTaggert is a genetics specialist and her work focuses on mutant affairs. She is shown in *X-Men: The Last Stand* in a video discussing whether it is ethical to transfer the mind of a man who is dying into the body of a brain-damaged man. The viewers are left wondering whether it is right to give the dying man a chance of being a father to his kids or whether it is morally wrong to give him the other man's body.

Moira has known Professor X for a long time and like many

mutants she admires what he achieved in his life. She sat next to Dr Hank McCoy (Beast) at his memorial; he shares her interest in genetics.

Later, she is shocked to find that Professor X has transferred his mind into the body of a man who was born without a fully functioning brain and has been lying in a coma. He didn't die when the Phoenix destroyed his body.

The actress Olivia Williams played Moira in *X-Men: The Last Stand* and Rose Byrne played a younger Moira in *X-Men: First Class*.

MR FANTASTIC

★ Appears in: *Fantastic Four* (2005), *Fantastic Four: Rise of the Silver Surfer* (2007)

★ Powers: His body is super-flexible and can be stretched into any desired shape

★ First comic-book appearance: November 1961

Reed Richards is a scientist and one of most intelligent men in the world. He was given the name Mr Fantastic after returning from a space mission with the ability to stretch his limbs. He falls in love with Sue Storm who is also a member of the Fantastic Four. They become man and wife in the second film.

Welsh actor Ioan Gruffudd played Reed in both films. Before being cast he was best known for playing Lancelot in *King Arthur* and between shooting *Fantastic Four* and its sequel he played William Wilberforce in *Amazing Grace*.

Because his elasticated limbs were added postproduction, Ioan had to imagine what it would look like when it was finished. He explained how acting in this way felt to the BBC: '[It's] quite hard and tedious. You need a lot of concentration and a lot of

imagination obviously, because I can't physically put my hand under a door or stretch for a bottle of wine 10 foot away!

'There were moments when I was pinching myself and asking what on earth was I doing, but you have to remind yourself that you're like a child again, playing in your back garden pretending that you're doing all these things again. And it works out fine.'

He went on: 'When you're out in the high seas doing *Hornblower*, or physically on the back of a horse in *King Arthur*, it's somewhat easier to get under the skin of the characters but this was probably my hardest acting job to date.'

DID YOU KNOW?

When Ioan gets recognised by little kids and they come up to him he'll sometimes say that the Invisible Woman is standing with him but she's too shy to say anything.

N IS FOR...

NICK FURY

✦ Appears in: *Iron Man* (2008), *Iron Man 2* (2010), *Captain America: The First Avenger* (2011), *The Avengers* (2012)

✦ Powers: Advanced fighter, trained in weaponry, excels at martial arts

✦ First comic-book appearance: May 1963

Nick Fury is the General of S.H.I.E.L.D., which is the Strategic Homeland Intervention, Enforcement and Logistics Division. He is the person putting together the Avengers and helps watch over what is happening to Tony Stark. He sends in Natasha Romanoff to work undercover for Tony.

The actor chosen to play Nick Fury was Samuel L. Jackson and he will be appearing in nine films in all. The Nick Fury in

the comic books had always been a white man so Samuel liked being the first-ever black man to play him. It's thought that Nick Fury will have his own solo film released in 2012.

His scene in *Iron Man* is right at the end after the credits, and when Samuel went to see the film for the first time with his agent they sat right through it and it ended at the credits. There had been a mix-up with the movie tape, so to make it up to him Samuel was sent his 30-second scene to watch at home.

NIGHTCRAWLER (KURT WAGNER)

Appears in: *X2* (2003)

Powers: Ability to teleport

First comic-book appearance: May 1975

Nightcrawler is a mutant with amazing agility and the power to teleport. He has blue skin covered in angelic symbols that he has cut into himself. He has a large tail that he uses as a weapon. When he teleports, a blue smoke trail follows his movements. He might look like a demon but he is a very strong Catholic.

After being brainwashed by Jason Stryker he tried to kill the President of the United States but was stopped seconds from stabbing him on the Oval Office's desk. He leaves the knife stuck in the desk with the message 'Mutant Freedom Now' written on a red ribbon attached to the handle.

Storm and Jean Grey bring him back to the Institute and he recovers from his ordeal. He later saves the lives of Rogue, Storm and Professor X.

The actor who played Nightcrawler was Alan Cumming. He enjoyed being in a movie with so many actors and the fun things they got up to when they weren't filming. Playing Nightcrawler was extremely hard work because he had to get up at 2am each

day for make-up so that he would be ready in time. This is one of the main reasons Nightcrawler was missed out of *X-Men: The Last Stand* – because Alan had hated the long make-up sessions they didn't want to put him through it again just for a few scenes.

O IS FOR...

THE ORACLE (BARBARA GORDON)

- Appears in: To date there have been no appearances of the Oracle in any TV show or film
- Powers: None
- First comic-book appearance: January 1967

The Oracle is an expert computer hacker with a photographic memory. Although she is confined to a wheelchair she can fight when needed using her upper body. She has not always been confined to a wheelchair. She was Batgirl for a while until the Joker shot her in the spine. Now she works alongside the Huntress, Power Girl and Black Canary.

The Oracle is an orphan but was raised by her uncle James Gordon. She sees everything that goes on in Gotham and passes on the information for her team to act upon.

P IS FOR...

THE PUNISHER (FRANK CASTLE)

⚜ Appears in: *The Punisher* (2004), *Punisher: War Zone* (2008)

⚜ Powers: Expert fighter with lots of weapons at his disposal

⚜ First comic-book appearance: February 1974

The Punisher was an FBI agent called Frank Castle whose whole family were slaughtered by a criminal called Howard Saint; he thought he had killed Frank, too, but he survived. Frank took on the identity of the Punisher and set about punishing people who deserve to be punished. First on his list were Howard Saint and his cronies.

The British/Irish actor Ray Stevenson was cast as the Punisher. He is best known for playing Titus Pullo in *Rome* and

Dagonet in *King Arthur*. The second *Punishe*r film was a reboot and saw him take on mobster boss Jigsaw and his brother Loony Bin Jim.

Q IS FOR...

QUICKSILVER (PIETRO MAXIMOFF)

Appears in: Various animated TV series

Powers: Super-fast, ability to create whirlwinds

First comic-book appearance: March 1964

Pietro has a twin sister called Wanda who is the Scarlet Witch. Their father is Magneto and their mother wanted to protect them from him so gave birth to them on Wundagore Mountain. They were raised by the gypsy Django Maximoff who they consider to be their father.

Pietro and his sister were seen as demons when they first started showing their mutant abilities. Pietro can run extremely

fast (175mph) and he can create whirlwinds and tornedoes just by spinning. He has inherited some aspects of Magneto's personality and can easily be angered. His sister has the ability to cause things to burst into flames and she can disrupt energy fields too.

At first Quicksilver and the Scarlet Witch fought with the X-Men but they felt a duty to fight for Magneto and his Brotherhood. They later decided that they wouldn't use their mutant abilities for evil and joined the Avengers when they needed new members.

Quicksilver also became the leader of the Knights of Wundagore.

R IS FOR...

RIPTIDE (JANOS QUESTED)

- Appears in: *X-Men: First Class* (2011)
- Powers: Spinning ability, can fire weapons from his own skin
- First comic-book appearance: October 1986

Riptide is a mutant who is very difficult to defeat in battle because of his ability to spin faster than a hurricane and fire blade-like spikes from his body. Nothing is strong enough to withstand his spikes and shurikens.

Álex González was the actor chosen to play Riptide in *X-Men: First Class*.

ROGUE (MARIE D'ANCANTO)

Appears in: *X-Men* (2000), *X2* (2003), *X-Men: The Last Stand* (2006)

Powers: Ability to absorb powers, strength and memories from those she touches

First comic-book appearance: 1981

Rogue is a mutant who wishes she wasn't. She was born a mutant but didn't realise she was one until she was teenager. She absorbs strength from any people or mutants she touches, their memories and, if they are mutants, their powers. She has no control over this and so has to keep her distance from people. She realised this when her boyfriend suffers a seizure after they kissed for the first time. Rogue is devastated because he could have died, and runs away. She abandons her human name Marie and becomes Rogue.

She meets Wolverine in a bar and ends up a lift hitching in his truck. They are getting on really well and then Sabretooth attacks. Thankfully Cyclops and Storm arrive at just the right time to help them. They take Rogue and Wolverine back to Xavier's Academy and Rogue finally finds somewhere she belongs. She makes friends with Bobby (Iceman) and Jon (Pyro). From the day she meets Wolverine he becomes like a father to her.

Whilst she is settling in Magneto decides that he needs her to power his machine that gives humans mutant abilities. He has been powering it himself but knows it could kill him. If he gets Rogue to absorb his powers she can take his place. He just needs to think of a way to capture her without Professor X being able to stop him. He gets Mystique to take the shape of Bobby and when the time is right say something to upset Rogue so she runs away. Magneto gets his wish when Rogue goes to wake Wolverine

and he accidentally stabs her with his claws. She touches Wolverine and although this allows her to heal it causes him to collapse. Mystique tells a horrified Rogue that Professor X is angry with her and Rogue decides she must leave.

Once Wolverine recovers he goes with a team to try and find her but Magneto snatches her. They manage to use Professor X's machine to find her location and head to the Statue of Liberty. They fight Magneto's mutants and manage to reach Rogue just in time. Cyclops takes on Magneto, injuring him, which allows Wolverine to destroy the machine and save Rogue who is close to death. He puts his hand on her face and she is able to use her powers to transfer his healing abilities. When he destroys the machine Rogue gets a white streak in her hair.

In the second film, Rogue starts to date Bobby who can turn his whole body and anything around him to ice.

William Stryker hates mutants and invades the X-Mansion but Rogue, Wolverine, Iceman and Pyro manage to escape and head for Iceman's childhood home. His brother tells the authorities where they are and they soon arrive on the scene. Wolverine is shot and Pyro gets so angry he starts attacking people. Rogue knows she needs to calm him down so touches him.

After showing great initiative and strength in battle Rogue and Iceman are later promoted to full X-Men alongside Storm, Cyclops and Wolverine.

In the third film, when it is announced that a mutant cure has been developed Rogue isn't as angry or upset as lots of her fellow mutants. She has always seen her abilities as being a curse and if she didn't have them she would be able to be physically close to Iceman. She is scared she is going to lose him because of the amount of time he is spending with Kitty Pryde. Iceman tries to stop her taking the cure but she goes ahead because it's what she's always wanted. Rogue thinks that the cure is permanent but it is suggested that it might not be so she could soon have her 'curse' back.

Rogue was played by Anna Paquin in all three films. She is a highly talented actress and won an Oscar when she was only 11 years old. She has gone on to play Sookie Stackhouse in the Emmy-winning series *True Blood*. She found working on the *X-Men* films completely different to anything she had done before. She explained to About.com: 'So little of the time that you actually spend on set has anything to do with the job that an actor does. You are waiting a lot for technical things to be set up and figured out. There's always going to be little hitches along the way, equipment not working the way it's supposed to. Just all these things that I don't really understand a lot about but have nothing to do with acting whatsoever. It just means it takes a really, really, really long time and [it] can be very long hours. But, there's also a lot of fun stuff that you get to do in those movies that you wouldn't get to do in any other straight, normal film.'

S IS FOR...

SHADOWCAT (KITTY PRYDE)

- Appears in: *X-Men* (2000), *X2* (2003), *X-Men: The Last Stand* (2006)
- Powers: Can phase herself and others
- First comic-book appearance: January 1980

Kitty is a mutant who has the phasing ability, which means she can pass through people and objects with ease. She can go through walls and floors as if they aren't even there; this freaked Wolverine out the first time he saw her walk through a wall. When Stryker attacked the school she was able to escape as she just kept running through walls and her potential captors. She helped Xaxier by getting some confidential government records for him, without anyone being aware of what she did.

She is close to Iceman, something which made Rogue jealous and helped her make her decision to take the mutant cure. Rogue couldn't bear the thought of Iceman choosing Kitty over her.

Whilst the mutants are fighting on Alcatraz Island, Kitty manages to reach Leech in his secure room before Juggernaut, but they can't escape because being close to Leech stops Kitty's phasing ability. The Brotherhood want to kill Leech because he is the source of the cure. Juggernaut busts his way in and runs straight at them. They move at just the right time and he ends up hitting his head so hard against the wall that he knocks himself out.

Several actresses have played Kitty. She was played by Sumela Kay in the first film, Katie Stuart in the second film and Ellen Page in the third film.

SPIDER-MAN

- Appears in: *Spider-Man* (2002), *Spider-Man 2* (2004), *Spider-Man 3* (2007), *The Amazing Spider-Man* (2012)
- Powers: 'Spider-sense', spider-like powers, strength, speed, heightened senses, ability to shoot web string from his wrists and to hang upside down
- First comic-book appearance: August 1962

Peter Parker was just a normal high-school student and then one day he was bitten by a genetically modified spider. He would never be the same again.

In the first film we get to see Peter before he transforms into Spider-Man. He is highly intelligent, especially when it comes to science, but he isn't good at mixing with other students. He's quite shy and his best friend is Harry Osborn. He lives with his

Uncle Ben and Aunt May, and he has a crush on the girl next door Mary Jane.

Harry's dad Dr Norman Osborn is very interested in Peter because he is so good at physics. In fact he shows more interest in Peter than he does his own son. He is extremely wealthy and is the CEO of his own company Oscorp. Oscorp is a company that manufactures chemicals and Norman wants them to supply chemical weapons to the US army but this puts him under immense pressure.

Peter, Harry, Mary Jane and the rest of their classmates go on a field trip to a genetics lab. During their visit a genetically modified spider escapes and bites Peter. He doesn't suffer any huge side effects until later when he's at home. He collapses but when he wakes up the next day and puts on his glasses he finds that his vision has gone really blurry. When he takes his glasses off he realises that it is the glasses that are causing the blurriness because his eyesight is perfect. He misses the bus as usual but manages to run super-fast and catch up with it. He notices at school that his skinny arms seem more toned, he can shoot webs from his wrists and his senses seem to be sharper than usual. He even manages to beat Mary Jane's boyfriend in a fight – something he would have run a mile from normally because the guy is so huge.

Peter realises that his new abilities must be down to the spider that bit him and, he decides to risk it all by going up onto a rooftop and jumping from one building to the next, and to learn to use his web strings to move around. Peter could have killed himself if his spider abilities hadn't kicked in.

Peter is so keen for Mary Jane to like him that he enters a wrestling tournament so he can buy a sports car. The rules of the tournament mean that he has to beat the reigning champion, but he is such a tough opponent that most people only manage to last a few seconds. Whoever beats him will earn $3,000. No one watching thinks Peter stands a chance and believes he could end

up seriously injuring himself. Peter knows he can do it but he doesn't tell his aunt and uncle. Ben drops Peter off thinking he has gone to the library to study. They have a minor disagreement in the car when Ben tries to give Peter some advice.

Peter puts on a costume he made himself and the boxing announcer gives him the name 'The Amazing Spider-Man'. He manages to win thanks to his incredible spider senses and skills. He goes backstage to meet the man in charge of the tournament but he will only give him $100. It seems he never expected anyone to beat his champion. As Peter is leaving a thief steals from the man who refused to give him any more money and Peter is glad, so he doesn't try to stop him. Once he gets outside he realises what he has done – the thief shot Uncle Ben as he was making his escape. His uncle dies and Peter feels like it's entirely his fault. He had ignored Ben's advice earlier when he was just trying to help and is haunted by his words: 'With great power comes great responsibility'.

Peter decides he needs to do something for the greater good with his powers and so will start fighting crime as Spider-Man. Soon the whole of New York is talking about him and the editor of the *Daily Bugle* is desperate to get photos of him to run alongside the stories he is printing. Peter comes up with the idea of being Spider-Man's official photographer. He can give his wages to Aunt May to help her with the bills.

Meanwhile at Oscorp, the army insist that the weapons Norman wants to supply to them are tested, so Norman becomes the guinea pig. The drugs give him superhuman strength but they mess with his head too, leaving him with a split personality. He kills his assistant and several of his rivals before contacting Spider-Man. He wears an armoured suit and uses a goblin glider to get around. He is the Green Goblin!

The Green Goblin plans to work with Spider-Man but he refuses. The Green Goblin isn't prepared to take no for an answer. When he discovers that Peter is Spider-Man he attacks

Aunt May, almost killing her. At the hospital Harry notices Mary Jane and Peter holding hands. He tells Norman and instantly his father knows that Mary Jane is Spider-Man's weakness.

He becomes the Green Goblin again and kidnaps Mary Jane, and a tram carriage full of school children. He dangles them both from the Queensboro Bridge and then drops them. He wants to test Spider-Man by seeing who he saves, Mary Jane or the children. Thankfully Spider-Man is able to save both and then continues his battle.

The fighting is intense and it looks like the Green Goblin is going to win until Spider-Man is able to use his web to pull down a wall on top of him. The Green Goblin gloats that he would be going after Mary Jane once he had killed Spider-Man, which makes Spider-Man angry enough to launch a counterattack. The Green Goblin tries to distract Spider-Man by revealing that he is Norman, and that the Green Goblin has been controlling him. As he is speaking he activates his goblin glider behind Spider-Man. Thankfully Spider-Man uses his spider sense to estimate when the glider will hit and jumps at just the right time. The glider flies into the Green Goblin, its sharp spikes ripping into his suit. In his final words he asks Spider-Man to not tell Harry that he was the Green Goblin.

Later, Peter (dressed as Spider-Man) carries Norman's battered body back to his mansion. He doesn't know it but Harry sees him. He wrongly thinks that Spider-Man killed his dad and at his funeral tells Peter that he plans to kill Spider-Man, not realising his friend and his enemy are the same person. Peter could easily have told Harry the truth, that his dad was the Green Goblin and was killed by his own glider, but he has made a promise, and he doesn't want his friend to suffer any more pain.

Peter loves Mary Jane but realises she will always be at risk if he dates her so tells her they should just be friends. He hates to see Mary Jane so upset but knows it is for the best. He has to keep her safe.

In the second film we see an exhausted Peter try to combine his university studies with being a superhero. He loses his pizza delivery job and doesn't even have Mary Jane to turn to as they are no longer close. Aunt May is scared she is going to lose her home because of financial troubles and even the *Daily Bugle* has started printing negative stories about Spider-Man.

Harry has taken over from his dad and is now in charge of Oscorp. He hires a scientist called Otto Octavius to come and work for him. Otto is a brilliant scientist and Peter has long been a fan of his. He takes too many risks, though, and when he performs an experiment in sustained fusion he ends up killing his wife and causing permanent damage to himself. Peter is part of a group that watches as Otto wearing several robotic arms that have artificial intelligence enters his experimental reactor. Warning messages flash up but Otto ignores them and the inhibitor chip which stops the mechanical arms from controlling his mind is destroyed. The arms are permanently fused with his spine and the old Otto will never be seen again.

The mechanical arm is now in charge and the arms start killing people that attempt to separate them from Otto. They utilise the worst aspects of Otto's character and make him obsessed with finishing his experiment, whatever the cost. The new Doctor Octopus busts the door off the bank's safe and it flies across the bank, narrowly missing Aunt May and Peter who are there to talk to someone about refinancing their home. Peter quickly jumps up and leaves so he can turn into Spider-Man. Aunt May is shocked and asks him not to leave her but he is already gone.

While Otto is sorting out the money bags he hears Spider-Man swinging towards him. He quickly uses his mechanical arms to launch money bags at him. He manages to kidnap Aunt May and she is left hanging from a window as Spider-Man and Otto fight. Thankfully Spider-Man saves her before she falls to her death, although Otto escapes.

Things continue to go wrong when he finds out that Mary Jane plans to marry an astronaut called John Jameson. Peter loves her so much and he would give anything for her to dump John for him. Harry has too much to drink and hits Peter; he is still really angry about what happened to his dad and still blames Spider-Man. He is jealous of the relationship Peter had with his dad, too.

Peter notices that his abilities have been playing up; he is very stressed by everything that is going on, so decides to stop being Spider-Man. He doesn't want to sacrifice his life and his happiness any more. Peter might be happier but the people of New York now start to suffer as the criminals realise that they no longer have to worry about Spider-Man showing up. Crime rises drastically and New York urgently needs its hero back.

Peter realises how much Spider-Man is needed when he rescues a girl from a fire only to find out that someone else died – if he'd been Spider-Man he could have saved both of them. Aunt May encourages him when she tells him that they need a hero, and that sometimes we have to give up on our dreams to help others.

Harry does a deal with Otto as he wants Spider-Man dead and Otto wants tritium for his experimental reactor. He tells Otto that Peter is the man who will be able to get him access to Spider-Man, not caring that he is putting Peter in danger. Peter and Mary Jane are chatting over coffee in a cafe when Otto strikes. He tells Peter that he wants Spider-Man to meet him at the Westside Tower at 3 o'clock or he will 'peel the flesh' off Mary Jane.

Peter puts on his Spider-Man suit, knowing that he has to rescue Mary Jane. He finds that his recent break has helped him and his abilities are back to full strength.

Otto is a tough opponent, with his multiple arms giving him numerous ways of attacking Spider-Man. They chase and fight each other all over New York, finally ending up on an elevated

train. Otto destroys the brakes and causes the train to travel at maximum speed. He tells Spider-Man he has a train to catch before jumping to safety. Spider-Man has to come up with a plan quickly because the line isn't finished and they will all fall to their deaths. He tries lowering his feet down onto the tracks to try and make the train slow down but it doesn't work. He then fires a web string from each wrist onto the nearby buildings, which looks like it will work until the strings pull the fronts off the buildings. Time is running out, so he blasts several web strings from each wrist and holds on to the ends of them, stretching himself to his limits. The train slows right down but after it hits the bumper blocks, the first carriage is left dangling over the edge. Spider-Man has stopped the train but it has sapped all of his strength. Only the hands of the people he has saved stop him from falling to his death as he collapses.

Otto returns and takes an exhausted Spider-Man to Harry before leaving. Harry unmasks him and is horrified to find that his best friend is Spider-Man, the person he hates most in the whole world. Peter quickly explains that they need to stop Otto because he has Mary Jane and they need to get to him before he finishes his experiment.

Harry lets him go and Peter rushes to the waterfront laboratory to save Mary Jane. He fights with Otto and they end up crashing through the floorboards and into the water underneath. Meanwhile, Otto's reactor starts drawing things into it; Mary Jane's chains are the only things stopping her but they soon start breaking. As she screams, Spider-Man leaves Otto and goes to save her, dragging her back with his web string. He tells her to run before Otto attacks again. The reactor is gaining so much power that it starts swallowing up the whole lab. Taxis from nearby streets start being pulled towards it. Spider-Man manages to give Otto an electric shock when he breaks the power cables but the reactor still keeps growing.

The mechanical arms fail because of the rush in electricity,

and lie in the pools of water that surround Otto. The old Otto resurfaces and recognises that Spider-Man is Peter Parker when he takes off his mask. Peter asks him to help stop the reactor but the arms grab hold of his neck. Peter appeals to the old Otto and tells him to not listen to his arms. Otto finally takes control and decides to drown the reactor, his dream. It is the only way to stop it because it has become self-sustaining.

Mary Jane sees Peter without his mask, and is almost crushed to death when the wall of the building collapses but Peter manages to hold it up. He is scared they might die and admits to Mary Jane that he loves her. He finds enough strength to lift the wall and they escape as the whole lab is submerged under water.

Afterwards Peter makes the brave decision to walk away again and tells her they can never be together. Harry sees his dad in a vision, telling him to avenge his death, and discovers his Green Goblin room. Mary Jane doesn't turn up at her own wedding and instead races across New York in her wedding dress to find Peter – she doesn't care what risks are involved, she wants to be with him.

In the third film Peter is feeling a lot happier than he used to and thinks he wants to marry Mary Jane. She is a Broadway actress and the public are once again enjoying having Spider-Man around. Things start to go wrong, though, when a meteorite crashes near New York and an organism from outerspace called a symbiote attaches itself to the back of Peter's moped.

A convict called Flint Marko gains superhuman abilities when he falls into a particle accelerator as he's trying to escape. The machine fuses his particles with the nearby sand, turning him into the Sandman. Harry decides to attack Spider-Man using the weapons he found in his dad's secret room. He hits his head during their fight, which causes him to lose part of his memory. He no longer wants to kill Spider-Man and can't remember unmasking him.

Spider-Man gets a shock when he tries to stop the Sandman

from stealing a car and finds out from the police that he is the man who killed Uncle Ben. Another man had gone to jail and died, but it turns out he was just Flint's accomplice. Spider-Man is going to have justice!

As Peter sleeps, the symbiote attaches to his Spider-Man costume and transforms it. No longer is it red and blue – it is black with a different Spider-Man symbol. It gives him better powers but makes him arrogant and self-obsessed. He fights with the Sandman and thinks he's killed him when he blasts him with water and turns him into mud.

Mary Jane notices the change in Peter and she doesn't like it one bit. Her acting career has taken a nosedive and she can't talk to Peter about how low she is feeling. She talks to Harry instead and he tells her to break it off with Peter. She does, telling him that she is in love with someone else. Peter is shocked when Harry turns up after Mary Jane leaves to reveal that he is her mystery man. The 'evil' side of Peter emerges thanks to his new suit and he attacks Harry.

Peter forgets about his morals and why he became Spider-Man in the first place. He changes his hairstyle and dresses differently. He also enjoys humiliating Eddie Brock at the *Daily Bugle* for faking photos of Spider-Man. He wants Mary Jane to regret dumping him and so takes Gwen on a date to the club where Mary Jane works. Gwen isn't impressed. Peter ends up getting in a fight with the club's doormen and pushes Mary Jane over. This makes Peter realise how much his new suit has changed him. He knows he has to do something so he can take it off because at the moment it is stuck to him and can't be removed. He goes to a church and sounds the church bells because the symbiote hates loud sounds.

Eddie Brock is sat in a pew praying to God to kill Peter because of how he humiliated him over the fake photos. He hears Peter's screams as he tries to remove the symbiote and goes to the bottom of the stairs that lead to the top of the tower. He

watches as it peels off Peter and falls from the church tower, landing next to him. It takes over his body, bringing him to his knees, and turns him into Venom.

Venom wants to kill Spider-Man because he knows it is Peter wearing the costume, and joins up with the Sandman who has recovered from Spider-Man's earlier attack. They kidnap Mary Jane and dangle her in a taxi over a building site using Venom's web strings. Peter realises that he will need help to rescue Mary Jane, so goes to Harry who initially has no intention of helping his former friend because he still thinks he killed his dad. Thankfully his butler is able to put him straight and explains what really happened. Harry now realises that Peter isn't a murderer and goes with him to help. Harry tries to control the Sandman whilst Spider-Man fights Venom.

Harry ends up sacrificing himself when Venom tries to kill Spider-Man with Harry's glider. The glider stabs him in the chest, just like the glider did to his dad during his fight with Spider-Man.

Spider-Man then uses the symbiote's hatred of loud noises to separate it from Eddie by using several pipes to pen Venom in and hitting them so they emit loud noises. Spider-Man throws one of Harry's bombs at the symbiote to destroy it and grabs Eddie, but the photographer wants the power the symboite gives him so much that he tries to get it to reattach to him. He ends up getting blown to pieces with the symbiote.

Harry had defeated the Sandman but Flint (the Sandman) had managed to tell Peter what really happened the night his Uncle Ben was killed. Uncle Ben had been trying to convince Flint to not steal the car when Flint's accomplice had returned and touched his arm. This made him shoot the gun without thinking, killing Uncle Ben. Flint had been so shocked that he hadn't gone with the other man in the car so hadn't been caught. Flint had regretted his actions ever since and only did the robbery to try and help his daughter who was dying and needed

urgent medical treatment to save her life. Hearing why Flint did it, and that he didn't mean to shoot his uncle, makes Peter forgive Flint, and all the hatred he had built up inside subsides. He watches as Flint disappears.

Peter and Mary Jane comfort Harry as he slips away and both Harry and Peter make amends for their past behaviours. Peter and Mary Jane decide to give things another go.

Tobey Maguire was the actor chosen to play Peter Parker and Spider-Man in the first three movies. The director had seen him play Homer Wells in *The Cider House Rules* and knew he would be perfect. The studio waited until they had seen him audition before they gave him the thumbs up.

Tobey talked to Cinema.com shortly after being cast for the first movie: 'I know that some people think I'm not exciting enough or volatile enough for this kind of role, but I think that kind of criticism is absolutely off-base. Peter Parker is not a typical action hero. He's probably the most down-to-earth, most carefully drawn, and least plastic of comic-book figures. For me, it's a role that I knew that I could pull off without disappointing people. And once people see the movie, I think they'll come to the same conclusion.'

He also talked about his fitness regime saying, 'I wasn't able to eat that much for a long time. But for someone like me who wasn't exactly a fitness freak, it was a chance of a lifetime to work with top trainers in different disciplines to get in great shape. I'm going to try to stay buff as long as I can, but it takes a lot of discipline and staying away from your favourite junk food!'

Tobey did such a great job that fans were shocked when the news broke that he wouldn't be playing Peter in *Spider-Man 4*. The studio wanted to go back to the beginning and explore how Peter got his powers, and how he juggled being a superhero with being a student. Tobey didn't take the news badly and said he was just glad he got to be in three great Spider-Man films.

Andrew Garfield will be playing Peter and Spider-Man in the new film, which is set to be released in July 2012. *The Amazing Spider-Man* is going to be released in 3-D and could turn out to be the best 3-D movie ever. Peter's love interest in this movie is going to be Gwen Stacy and the villain is going to be the Lizard.

STORM (ORORO MUNROE)

 Appears in: *X-Men* (2000), *X2* (2003), *X-Men: The Last Stand* (2006)

Powers: Ability to control and create the weather she desires

First comic-book appearance: 1975

Storm is a mutant who has the ability to control and create weather using her mind. She can cause lightning to strike and create whirlwinds if needed. She is one of the first X-Men and her eyes turn white when she uses her powers. Traditionally, she originates from Kenya and in the first film Halle Berry spoke with a Kenyan accent, but this was dropped in the next two films. She works at Professor X's school as a teacher but fights when needed. She is a mother figure for lots of the younger students in the school. Storm is a great asset to have on the X-Men team because of her powers.

She is a compassionate person but hates the way some people treat mutants. She becomes a friend of Nightcrawler in the second film.

Oscar winner Halle Berry played Storm in the first three films. She talked to Sci-fi Online about the type of woman Storm is. She said: 'I think Storm is a really strong woman who has great moral and ethical fibre. She is a warrior, in the sense that she will fight for what she believes in. She will say exactly

what she thinks, even if it does not represent the majority view. I think she is that kind of lady.'

Talking about the third film, she said: 'In this movie she gets to express her voice, she actually goes toe to toe with Wolverine and I think that is pretty impressive for Storm, because in the past X–Men films, she hasn't challenged anybody. This time there is a much more interesting dynamic between them and she is more assertive.

'In one scene she challenges Wolverine's beliefs and asks him to "Step up to the plate or step off". She will not accept any of his indecisiveness and she tells him that he has to make a choice. She is almost saying, "Make a choice, I don't even care what it is as long as you make one, because I need to know which side you are on."'

SUPERGIRL (KARA ZOR-EL)

 Appears in: *Supergirl* (1984), *Smallville* TV series

Powers: Same as Superman: super-strength, agility, ability to fly, X-ray vision, heat vision, heightened senses, invulnerability

First comic-book appearance: August 1958

Supergirl is the cousin of Superman. She was sent with Kal-El (Superman) from Krypton before it was destroyed. She was supposed to look after him but during the meteor shower that bought them to Earth she was trapped under a dam and stayed there for 18 years. By the time she is freed and finds Kal-El he a grown 'man' and because she hasn't aged during her period of suspended animation she looks very similar to him in age. She isn't used to dealing with humans and regularly says the wrong things. Clark often has to step in and look after her, even though she is the one who is supposed to be looking after him.

The actress Laura Vandervoort plays her in *Smallville*. She had to do a screen test for the role with a sprained ankle but still did enough for the casting people to pick her.

DID YOU KNOW?

- Laura his a second-degree black belt, so she was able to use her martial arts skills during the fight scenes.
- There was a *Supergirl* film, which was released in 1984, but it didn't do well and there hasn't been another one since.

SUPERMAN (CLARK KENT)

Appears in: *Superman and the Mole Men* (1951), *Superman: The Movie* (1978), *Superman II* (1981), *Superman III* (1983), *Supergirl* (1984), *Superman IV: The Quest for Peace* (1987), *Superman Returns* (2006), *Superman: Man of Steel* (2012)

Powers: super-strength, agility, ability to fly, X-ray vision, heat vision, heightened senses, invulnerability

First comic-book appearance: June 1938

Clark Kent was originally called Kal–El and came from the planet Krypton. He was sent away when he was a baby shortly before it was destroyed. He arrived on Earth during a meteor shower and was found by Martha and Jonathan Kent. They brought Clark up on their farm and never told anyone about his special abilities. Clark is super–strong, has never been ill and can fly (although he didn't realise he could until he was an adult). His one weakness is Kryptonite. Martha wanted Clark to use his powers for good and made him his Superman costume.

When he grows up he leaves his hometown of Smallville and

moves to Metropolis where he gets a job as a reporter for the *Daily Planet*. He wears glasses so he can keep his Superman identity a secret from everyone, especially his co-worker, Lois Lane.

Because there have been so many Superman movies and TV series the character and his story have changed from time to time. His biggest enemies are Lex Luthor and General Zod. The most famous Superman to date has been the one portrayed by Christopher Reeve. He played Superman in four films and sadly died in 2004 aged 52. His widow thought that Brandon Routh, the actor chosen to play Superman in the 2006 movie, looked a lot like her husband. *Superman Returns* was a different type of Superman film; Superman had been missing for five years before returning and it was revealed that Lois had given birth to his son whilst he was away, although she pretended that he was the son of her fiancé Richard White for the majority of the movie.

The new Superman movie is due to be released in 2012 and will be a reboot, so we will see Clark growing up in Kansas before he becomes Superman. He will be played by British actor Henry Cavill and Zack Snyder will be the director.

DID YOU KNOW?

Actor Nicolas Cage is such a big Superman fan that he named his son Kal-El.

T IS FOR...

THE THING (BEN GRIMM)

- Appears in: *Fantastic Four* (2005), *Fantastic Four: Rise of the Silver Surfer* (2007)
- Powers: Super-strength, hard to injure due to rock-like skin, ability to hold his breath for long periods
- First comic-book appearance: November 1961

Ben Grimm is an astronaut who becomes The Thing after being exposed to a cosmic cloud whilst in outer space. He has super-strength and looks like he has been made out of rocks. He also has a great sense of humour but is despodent over the change in his appearance.

At first Ben hates being The Thing because the woman he loves won't accept him. He decides he doesn't want to be a

member of the Fantastic Four or have his powers any more, so accepts Victor von Doom's offer to turn him back into just a normal man. Because losing his powers turns Victor into Doctor Doom, Ben has a hard decision to make. Doctor Doom is trying to kill his friends and Ben can't help them if he stays a man. He bravely decides to use Victor's machine to give him his powers back. After they defeat Doctor Doom, Ben accepts that he is The Thing and finds a woman who loves him for who he is, Alicia Masters.

The actor Michael Chiklis played The Thing in both films but it is thought that a new actor will be chosen to play him in the reboot movie.

THOR

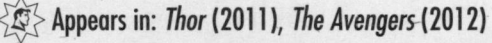 Appears in: *Thor* (2011), *The Avengers* (2012)

 Powers: Super-strength, speed, stamina, agility, can travel through time, fly, defect bullets with his hammer, almost indestructible, never tires, can cause lightning to strike, create rain, snow, wind...and many more

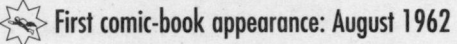 First comic-book appearance: August 1962

Thor is a god and is the son of Odin. He is incredibly strong and he can fly. He is a great warrior and can' throw lightning bolts. His weapon is his hammer. His adopted brother is Loki.

Loki resented Thor from a young age because of the way others treated them differently. They approved of Thor's strength and bravery in battles but dismissed Loki because he wasn't able to do everything Thor could; instead Loki's strengths lay in sorcery. Now Loki's anger has grown and all he wants is power and revenge. He hates Thor with a passion and vows to destroy mankind.

Thor is sent to Earth by Odin because he is so arrogant and full of himself that he reignites an ancient war between the gods. His father thinks being cast to Earth will punish Thor for what he has done. He doesn't think Thor has what it takes to take his place one day.

Thor learns from the humans he comes into contact with and they change his outlook on life. He won't let his brother destroy them. He is particularly fond of astrophysicist Jane Foster.

The actor chosen to play Thor in both movies was Chris Hemsworth. Chris was previously most famous for playing George Kirk in the movie *Star Trek* but Thor will become his biggest role.

Chris was asked by MoviesOnline what his take on Thor is. Chris replied: 'He's a brash, cocky young warrior and he's got to learn some humility. It's about that journey. I think him learning to temper what is his greatest strength is also his biggest danger, which is that power.'

He also talked about the stunts and fight scenes: 'I love that stuff… you know, there's something I thought I could do and I couldn't, which was being strapped into this harness and I had to pretend like I was falling through space. I basically was there on a couple of wires and they just spin you. You spin backwards. I thought that's something that at the show grounds you pay five bucks for and it's just going to be fun. Two spins later, I was like whooooaaaaa. We stopped and I was like pale. They're like, "You want to stop?" I was like, "No, just keep going until I throw up I guess." He just kept spinning and going, "You all right, Chris?" It's like (gasps), "Go again, go again." Eventually we got what we needed and I just had to sit down for a couple hours. It was hideous.'

DID YOU KNOW?
One of Chris's brothers auditioned for Thor, too, but didn't get the part.

U IS FOR...

ULTRA BOY (JO NAH)

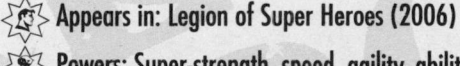 Appears in: Legion of Super Heroes (2006)

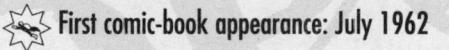 Powers: Super-strength, speed, agility, ability to fly, invulnerability, flash vision, penetra-vision (allows him to see through anything — even lead)

First comic-book appearance: July 1962

Ultra Boy comes from the planet Rimbor and gained his powers after the spaceship he was travelling in was swallowed up by a gigantic space creature. He ate some of the creature and was given ultra-powers. He has super-strength, super-speed, the ability to fly, invulnerability and freezing breath. The only drawback is that he can only use one of his powers at a time, so he needs to pick the right one depending on the situation he faces.

At the Intergalactic Games he is racing against the Lightning Lad and other fast superheroes when they are attacked by the Fatal Five. He uses four of his powers as he fights alongside Kem of Bismoll and Phantom Girl.

The voice of Jo Nah in the *Legion of Super Heroes* was provided by James Arnold Taylor. James is a very famous voice actor and he has lent his voice to Fred Flintstone and Obi-Wan Kenobi.

V IS FOR...

VIXEN (MARI JIWE MCCABE)

- Appears in: *Justice League Unlimited Animated Series*
- Powers: Takes the abilities of animals
- First comic-book appearance: July 1981

Mari comes from Africa but now lives in New York. Her family were passed down an ancient totem, which has the power to give whoever wears it amazing animal powers. Her evil uncle killed her father for the totem but Mari managed to take it back.

She works as a model in New York but also uses the totem's powers to become Vixen. In order to gain the abilities of a particular animal she just focuses on it. She has claws which help her in battle and can heal herself just by touching her injuries. Vixen joins the Justice League.

W IS FOR...

WAR MACHINE (COL. JAMES 'RHODEY' RHODES)

✦ Appears in: *Iron Man* (2008), *Iron Man 2* (2010)

✦ Powers: When wearing the suit he is super strong, able to fly, can fire repulsor beams and has advanced weaponry

✦ First comic-book appearance: January 1979

Col. James 'Rhodey' Rhodes is in the US Air Force. He is Tony Stark's best friend (aside from Pepper Potts) but also works with him on a professional basis as he is the person who deals with Stark Industries' weapons division. They have known each other for many years and even went to college together.

When Tony discovers that the terrorists that captured him are

using his weapons, given to them by Obadiah Stane, to destroy the Afghan village of the man who helped him escape, he heads there straight away – in his new suit. He soon defeats them but as he attempts to fly out of the country he runs into trouble and is deemed a risk by the US Air Force who are patrolling the skies. They decided to attack him using two F-22 Raptor jets. Tony ends up calling Rhodey who has the power to stop the attack, but he escapes anyway without needing his friend's help. Rhodey knows Tony really well but he can't believe the risks he has just taken. He should report him to his superiors but Rhodey doesn't want to get Tony in trouble.

Obadiah has had his own Iron Man-style suit made but needs an arc reactor to power it. He breaks into Tony's home, attacks him, rips out his arc reactor and leaves Tony to die. Thankfully, Rhodey arrives at just the right time and manages to help an incredibly weak Tony insert his very first arc reactor into his chest. Tony then puts on his Iron Man suit and blasts through the roof to rescue Pepper and apprehend Obadiah. Without Rhodey he would certainly have died and Obadiah would have gained full control of Stark Industries.

After Obadiah dies and the world learns that Tony is Iron Man, Rhodey is given the task of keeping an eye on him. The military demand Tony hands over his suit and the Iron Man technology to them but he refuses. They do get their hands on one of Tony's suits, though, when Rhodey takes it after Tony's birthday party shenanigans. Tony got so ridiculously drunk in his Iron Man suit that Rhodey had to put on a suit himself to try and calm things down. He kicks everyone out of the party and then he and Tony fight.

The suit is given to Justin Hammer so he can use it to build his own drones, which he decides to unveil at the Stark Expo. Rhodey joins them on stage in his war hammer suit and things go to plan until Ivan Venko starts to control them via remote control. Rhodey can't stop himself from attacking Tony in his

Iron Man suit; he can only watch and hope that his friend manages to escape. Thankfully Happy and Natalie/Natasha manage to give Rhodey control over his War Machine suit again after breaking into Hammer's headquarters. He quickly finds Iron Man and together they take on Ivan. They manage to defeat him by firing repulsor rays at each other, which damages Ivan's suit beyond repair. He is virtually powerless but decides to activate the self-destruct device that blows up himself and the drones. The blast destroys the Stark Expo complex but War Machine and Iron Man survive to fight another day.

Rhodey ends up receiving a bravery medal from Senator Stern alongside Tony and it's clear that Iron Man has a new sidekick in War Machine.

Two actors have played Rhodey so far. Terrence Howard played him in *Iron Man* and Don Cheadle played him in the sequel and will be playing him in the third movie. Terrence was due to play him in *Iron Man 2* but there were issues over the contract and in the end the studio looked for a new actor to play Rhodey and cast Don Cheadle.

Don explained to IGN what happened. He said: 'I got a phone call from my agent saying they were offering me the part. That was kind of it. It happened very fast, and I had a very short time to answer. Literally, overnight. I was unaware of what was happening with Terrence. And when they called me I asked what was going on with Terrence. I've worked with Terrence; I've known Terrence for a long time. And they said they were moving away from him. So it's not like I was taking Terrence's job, because the job was already gone. Someone else was going to do the part. I don't know who the next person in line was, but that's what they were going to.'

WOLVERINE (JAMES LOGAN)

Appears in: *X-Men* (2000), *X2* (2003), *X-Men: The Last Stand* (2006), *X-Men Origins: Wolverine* (2009)

Powers: Incredible strength, virtually unstoppable, claws in each hand, formidable fighter

First comic-book appearance: October 1974

Wolverine's past was explored in *X-Men Origins: Wolverine*. His real name is James Logan and he has a half-brother called Victor. They didn't realise they were brothers until James killed the man who he saw murder his father, only to find out that the second man was his real father – meaning that Victor was his half-brother. He killed him using the claws that grow from his hands when he is angry. He already knew as a child that he was different, and a mutant.

Up until that point he had thought that his name was James Howlett. James and Victor's father was a cruel man who had treated Victor appallingly and that is why he decided to run away with James.

James and Victor became soldiers fighting in various wars side by side. James was the leader out of the two of them. Things were going good until Victor tried to rape a woman in Vietnam, which resulted in him being sentenced to death alongside James (he stepped in to help his brother as he was being attacked by soldiers). James and Victor faced a firing squad but no normal bullet can penetrate their skin. They were visited in their cell by Major Stryker who invited them to join a special team of mutants he was putting together. It was better than staying locked up in a prison cell so they agreed.

James and Victor have always had disagreements because they are very different men, but they have always stuck together. One

day this changes because James isn't prepared to be involved in a group that kills innocent civilians, and he walks away from Team X. Victor refuses to leave. He has always been the more violent, bloodthirsty brother and he likes working for William Stryker.

James tries to leave his mutant side behind him and starts using the name Logan. He falls in love with Kayla Silverfox, who he believes to be a non-mutant. Years pass and they build a life together. Things couldn't be better until Stryker turns up to warn Logan that someone is hunting down members of Team X and killing them. Logan believes he knows who the murderer is when he finds Kayla's body. Logan thinks Victor has murdered the woman he loves. They fight but Logan can't beat Victor; he is too strong.

Stryker offers Logan a way to make sure that next time he meets his brother in battle he can beat him. Logan agrees to let Stryker bond the metal adamantium with his skeleton to make him an unbeatable force. As the procedure is taking place Wolverine overhears Stryker mention to Agent Zero that his memory should be erased and quickly escapes.

Logan has taken on the name Wolverine after a tale Kayla told him about the moon and its lover. He wants to know where Stryker's new lab is and tracks down the only member of Team X he trusts, John Wraith. He manages to speak to Remy LeBeau who is the only mutant to have escaped from the lab, and after convincing him that he isn't about to capture him and send him back, he is shown where to go.

Once he arrives he discovers his brother, Stryker and Kayla. It turns out that it was all a set-up. Kayla is a mutant and she was given the task of making him fall in love with her. They staged her death so that he would agree to Stryker's experiment. Wolverine is devastated even though Kayla explains that she had to do it because Stryker is holding her sister captive and he promised to release her if Kayla did as he said. He went back on his promise.

Wolverine leaves but ends up returning when he hears Kayla

screaming. Victor is furious after finding out the promise Stryker made to him about adding adamantium to his spine was a lie; Stryker says it would kill him. Kayla tries to tell Victor that his boss has tricked them both but this just makes Victor want to kill her. Wolverine fights Victor but stops short of killing him after Kayla convinces him not to.

Stryker sets Weapon XI/Deadpool on Wolverine. He used to be called Wade Wilson and was in Team X but he is virtually unrecognisable now. Stryker gave him all the mutant abilities Victor had collected when he killed the other members of Team X as well as the abilities of the young mutants he had been experimenting on. Wolverine struggles against Deadpool because of his teleporting and vast array of other abilities. Thankfully, Victor decides to help because he doesn't want to let anyone else kill his brother. Wolverine manages to slice off Deadpool's head and push him off the cooling tower. His brother leaves once the battle is over.

Wolverine carries an injured Kayla to safety with the other mutant captives but Stryker reappears and shoots him in the head with adamantium bullets. Kayla controls Stryker's mind and tells him to drop the gun and keep walking, even when his feet bleed. She then dies but Wolverine survives as his body heals itself, although his memory has been damaged and he doesn't recognise Kayla when he sees her dead body. He can't remember his past or the fact that Victor is his brother.

There is a second *Wolverine* movie due to be released in 2012. Not much is known about the plot so far apart from the fact that Wolverine visits Japan and is taught by a samurai warrior.

In the *X-Men* movie, Rogue chats to Wolverine in a bar after watching him take part in a cage fight. Rogue notices his claws and realises that he is a mutant like her. She asks if she can travel with him in his truck and at first he refuses. He is used to travelling alone. In the end he agrees and says she can. They are getting on really well when Sabretooth (Victor) attacks. Thankfully Cyclops

and Storm arrive at just the right time to help them. They take Rogue and Wolverine back to the X-Mansion. Wolverine has never met so many mutants before and decides to stick around after Professor X tells him he could learn more about his past by staying. He might be able to learn to have more control over his claws, too.

Wolverine remains close to Rogue and he takes on a fatherly role. He enjoys spending time with Jean Grey and winding up her boyfriend Cyclops.

Whilst Wolverine and Rogue are settling into life at the X-Mansion, Magneto is building a machine that gives humans mutant abilities. He has been powering it himself but knows it could kill him. He knows about Rogue's ability to absorb the powers of any mutant she touches so decides he needs to capture her without Professor X or anyone else being able to stop him. He gets Mystique to take the shape of Bobby and when the time is right say something to upset Rogue so she runs away. Magneto gets his wish when Rogue goes to wake Wolverine and he accidentally stabs her with his claws. She touches Wolverine and although this allows her to heal it causes him to collapse. Mystique tells a horrified Rogue that Professor X is angry with her and Rogue decides she must leave.

Once Wolverine recovers he goes with a team to try and find her but Magneto snatches her. They manage to use Professor X's machine to find her location and head to the Statue of Liberty. They fight Magneto's mutants and manage to reach Rogue just in time. Cyclops takes on Magneto, injuring him, which allows Wolverine to destroy the machine and save Rogue who is close to death. He puts his hand on her face and she is able to use her powers to transfer his healing abilities. This could kill him but he thinks it's worth the risk.

His plan works and Rogue is brought back to full fitness. Wolverine is taken back to the X-Mansion and has to recover because letting Rogue absorb his healing powers was very dangerous. Once he is better Professor X tells him that the

Alkali Lake has something to do with his past and so Wolverine decides to go there straight away. He gives Rogue his dogtags and tells her he will be back.

In *X2*, Wolverine finds the Alkali Lake and the empty factory next to it. He expected to find a lot more and is left feeling crushed. Professor X sends him a message asking him to return to the X-Mansion, so he does. He is put in charge of the mutant students whilst Professor X and Cyclops go to visit Magneto in prison. They want to know what information William Stryker has got from the leader of the Brotherhood. Storm and Jean aren't around either because they have gone to find Nightcrawler who has been brainwashed by Stryker and his son Jason. Stryker captures Cyclops and Professor X but Wolverine doesn't know this.

As he's trying to sleep, Wolverine has nightmares about his past and the Weapon X programme. He goes for a walk because he can't get the images out of his head but at the same time doesn't understand what they mean. All of a sudden Stryker and his men break into the Mansion and start looking for Professor X's Cerebro machine. Wolverine fights back, killing many, as he won't let Stryker hurt any of the students. He tells Rogue, Iceman, Pyro and Colossus to go and joins them in the car a few minutes later. Seeing Stryker has brought more memories to the forefront of his mind: could he have had something to do with his past?

They head to Iceman's (Bobby's) childhood home in Boston and are soon joined by Storm, Nightcrawler and Jean who arrive in the X-Jet. Bobby's brother alerts the authorities out of jealousy and they have to fight their way out. Magneto and Mystique offer to help them defeat Stryker and rescue Professor X. They know that Stryker has the Cerebro and that he is planning on using it to kill all the mutants. The two teams join up because they need each other and are stronger together. They head to the Alkali Lake to tackle Stryker.

Wolverine might have started flirting with Jean harmlessly in

the beginning but he genuinely loves her now. He kisses her but she tells him that she loves Scott (Cyclops). Mystique sees this and decides to take the shape of Jean. Later she enters Wolverine's tent and tries to pretend 'she' has changed her mind. Wolverine can't be fooled and realises that it is Mystique when he sees a scar on her stomach from when he stabbed her during their fight at the Statue of Liberty.

Once they are ready to infiltrate Stryker's base, Mystique takes the shape of Wolverine and manages to get Stryker's men to let the other X-Men in. They split up and Wolverine finds himself in a lab that has his claw marks on the walls. Seeing the marks makes him finally remember how Stryker experimented with him and bonded adamantium to his skeleton. He is soon joined by Stryker who admits he is the one that created the 'animal within' him. He wasn't the only mutant Stryker experimented on: he performed a similar procedure on Yuriko Oyama (Deathstrike). Wolverine is forced to fight her and only manages to win by injecting her with adamantium.

Wolverine goes after Stryker because he wants more answers. He needs to know about his past. Stryker refuses to tell him what he wants and Wolverine ends up leaving him to die. Magneto had chained Stryker to some debris and when the dam breaks it will kill him.

Wolverine is devastated that Jean was killed as she protected them from the water when the dam broke. Cyclops can't believe she has gone either, and is comforted when Wolverine tells him Jean wanted to be with Cyclops not him.

In X-Men: The Last Stand Wolverine has a hard decision to make because Jean has become Phoenix and this side of her personality is too dangerous. She kills Professor X and joins Magneto, but still Wolverine loves her. As the X-Men battle against Magneto's Brotherhood on Alcatraz Island Wolverine has to do something because the Phoenix is out of control, and only he is able to get close to her because he has the power to heal.

He begs Jean/the Phoenix to stop but she won't. Then the Jean part of her surfaces and asks him to stop the Phoenix. Wolverine declares his love for her and then stabs her. She is later buried alongside Cyclops and Professor X.

The actor who plays Wolverine in all the movies is Hugh Jackman. He wasn't the person originally cast – scottish actor Dougray Scott was given the part, but when *Mission Impossible II* overran by two months, he had to pull out and Hugh was given the job instead. Hugh was an unusual choice because he was better known as a theatre actor than a movie actor and he was far too tall. Hugh is 6ft 2½ and Wolverine is meant to be a small guy, at 5ft 3. Hugh's wife didn't think that Wolverine was the right part for him but he still went for it, and he is so glad now that he did because it turned him into a huge star. He found it quite hard preparing to play Wolverine for the first time because he had to practice wearing claws and he wasn't very good at it. His body has quite a few scars because of it!

DID YOU KNOW?

The premiere for *X-Men Origins: Wolverine* took place in Tempe, Arizona after its residents won the chance to host it. Hugh ordered coffee and pastries for 800 *X-Men* fans who had camped out overnight to catch a glimpse of the stars on the red carpet.

The Wolverine portrayed in the *Origins* movie was different to the Wolverine in the three *X-Men* movies because Hugh wanted to get back to a Wolverine that the fans wanted. He revealed all to Crave Online: 'About every third day, for the rest of your life, you hear a critique about how you played the part, what you should have done differently, and what you can do the next time, if you ever get a shot at it. I knew exactly what fans wanted, and not just the comic-book fans but fans of the movie'.

'It's fair to say that, by *X-Men 3*, Wolverine had gone a little soft, and I agree with them there. What fans love about Wolverine is his more uncompromising approach to life. He is who he is. He's not always a nice guy. He has got edge. He's an anti-hero. And, there's also a vulnerability in there. There is conflict and battles going on in there. With Gavin [Hood, the director] and the other actors, I had the chance to explore that more. I wanted the film to feel different. Gavin and I talked a lot about the aesthetic and tone of it. It's a little darker, a little rawer, a little tougher and, hopefully, maybe even a little more human. That's really what has appealed to me about the comic book. And, no more black leather suits.'

WONDER WOMAN (DIANA PRINCE)

 Appears in: *Wonder Woman* TV series

Powers: Has abilities given to her by the Olympian Gods, can communicate with animals, is an expert when it comes to using the bow and arrow and sword

First comic-book appearance: 1941

Wonder Woman is an Amazon with amazing strength, agility, stamina and the ability to fly. Her weapons are the lasso of truth, her bracelets and her tiara. She becomes Diana Prince so that she can keep her real identity a secret. Diana works as a secretary for the military so she can learn things she can use when she's Wonder Woman. Unlike Clark Kent who is super-strong all the time, Diana doesn't have her powers until she becomes Wonder Woman.

She has only appeared in TV series and an animated movie so far, but there is a Wonder Woman movie planned for 2013 and a totally new nemesis is being created. In the past there have been lots of attempts to make a Wonder Woman film, with Sandra Bullock having been one of the actresses considered to play her.

X IS FOR...

XAVIER (PROFESSOR X)

Appears in: *X-Men* (2000), *X2* (2003), *X-Men: The Last Stand* (2006), *X-Men Origins: Wolverine* (2009), *X-Men: First Class* (2011)

Powers: Psionic abilities, can fire mental blasts at opponents

First comic-book appearance: September 1963

Xavier's full name is Professor Charles Francis Xavier but it is often shortened to Professor X. He is the leader of the X–Men and is a scientific genius. His special mutant abilities include telepathy and he is one of the best there has ever been at reading and controlling minds. He is confined to a wheelchair but this doesn't hold him back. He built Cerebro so he could track the location of mutants when he needs to. His biggest enemy is his

former childhood friend Magneto, who wants mutants to go to war against the humans.

In *X-Men*, Professor X senses when Wolverine and Rogue are being attacked by Sabretooth and sends Cyclops and Storm to save them and bring them back to the X-Mansion. The X-Mansion is Professor X's home, a base for the X-Men and the location of Xavier's school for young mutants. Professor X teaches his pupils how to control their powers and ultimately how to uses their gifts for good. He welcomes Rogue and Wolverine to stay with them – initially believing they were attacked because Magneto wants Wolverine when in reality it was Rogue he was targeting. Wolverine might not know anything about his past but Professor X does.

When Rogue runs away after being tricked by Mystique, Professor X uses Cerebro to find that she is at the train station so that Cyclops, Storm and Wolverine can try and save her. When they fail to bring her back he uses it again but it poisons him and causes him to go into a coma. His X-Men manage to stop Magneto's plan and rescue Rogue, and Professor X manages to recover. For a while it looked like he would die. He tells Wolverine to visit Alkali Lake to learn more about his past, which he does in *X2*.

Professor X is shocked when one of his own X-Men, Nightcrawler, is brainwashed into attempting to kill the President. He thinks Magneto might be behind the attack but it turns out it was Stryker and his son. Magneto had been brainwashed into telling them all about Cerebro and Professor X's school.

Stryker kidnaps Professor X and Cyclops and decides they need to be brainwashed, too. Professor X has a device fitted to him that stops him using his telepathic powers while Stryker's son Jason puts images into his head to control him. Stryker needs Professor X to control his own Cerebro so he can kill all the mutants. His plan works until the X-Men, Magneto and

Mystique arrive to stop him. Rather than just freeing Professor X, Magneto decides to use it himself. He gets Mystique to take the form of Stryker and then convinces Jason to make Professor X use the machine to kill all humans. Thankfully Nightcrawler and Storm are able to stop this from happening by freeing Professor X from Jason's control.

In *X-Men: The Last Stand* Professor X tries to help Cyclops who is struggling to cope after Jean's death. Professor X is devastated when Cyclops is killed by Jean/the Phoenix at Alkali Lake. He sends Wolverine and Storm to see what has happened and they return to the X-Mansion with an unconscious Jean. They couldn't find any sign of Cyclops, only his visor. Professor X was so close to Cyclops that it feels like he has lost a son. He instructs Storm that she should take over the school if anything happens to him in the future.

He sedates Jean to keep her safe and Wolverine watches over her. The Professor admits that he realised how potentially powerful Jean Grey was when she came to the school and decided to protect her by putting mental barriers up in her mind to control her powers. This resulted in her developing a second personality, the Phoenix, which only showed herself when Jean lost her powers as the water from the dam crashed over her.

When she wakes she manages to render Wolverine unconscious and heads for the home she grew up in as a child. Both Professor X and Magneto head there to try and get her to listen to them. Professor X insists he wants to help her control her powers and that he only created the mental barriers to try and protect her all those years ago. Magneto says that Professor X wants to control her and wants to cure her, in the hope that she will decide to join the Brotherhood. Professor X tries to get inside her head and this makes her really angry. She is extremely disorientated and when Professor X mentions Cyclops' death she turns into the Phoenix.

Professor X and the Phoenix use telepathy to fight each other

and she causes objects around them to disintegrate and gravity to flip. She no longer cares about Professor X and lifts him up along with the house. She doesn't want him in her head any more. His last words to her are: 'Don't let it control you.' Wolverine witnesses Professor X's final moments before he breaks up into small particles and the house crashes to the ground. Phoenix leaves with Magneto.

After the credits a scene was shown that implied that Professor X's mind had been transferred into the body of a man in a coma and wasn't killed by the Phoenix, after all.

DID YOU KNOW?

The man in a coma that Professor X speaks through is actually his identical twin brother who suffered in the womb because of Professor X being a mutant. When they were born his brother didn't have a fully functioning brain.

In *X-Men Origins: Wolverine*, Professor X helps the young mutants escape from the lab by speaking to Cyclops telepathically and leading them to safety. When they get outside he takes them via helicopter to his school. He was supposed to feature in *X-Men Origins: Magneto* but the movie was never made and he will instead be in *X-Men: First Class*.

The actor chosen to play Professor X in the first four movies was Sir Patrick Stewart, OBE. He was best known for playing Captain Jean-Luc Picard in *Star Trek: The Next Generation* before being cast as Professor X. He was replaced by James McAvoy for *X-Men: First Class* because the movie explores the beginnings of the X-Men.

James talked to Collider.com in January 2011 about how *X-Men: First Class* is living up to what he imagined it to be. He said: 'It's pretty much what I thought it would be when

Matthew [Vaughn, the director] took me through it all. He really wanted to play off the '60s setting of it, and play off the style of that, visually, in the design of the costumes and all that, which we totally got. And, he wanted us to be really free, in terms of characterisation, and was confident in taking it as far away from the original characters, not as we could, but as we thought was right.'

He went on: 'There's no point in doing a prequel, if they're just the exact same people. They've got to be very different; otherwise there is no journey. This story is all about that journey to showing the seeds of how they are in the other X-Men movies, and to show what could have been between Charles and Erik – or Professor X and Magneto – and to show why it couldn't be.'

The film was the biggest movie James had made in so little time – they knew when it was going to come out before they had even finished filming it. This meant that he had to work very long days with hardly any time off, and the actors couldn't afford to make many mistakes. James loved playing Professor X but was a bit disappointed that having the power of telepathy didn't allow him to do some of the crazy stunts the other actors got to do.

Y IS FOR...

YOUNG AVENGERS

 Appears in: To date there have been no appearances of the Young Avengers in any TV show or film

Powers: Various

First comic-book appearance: April 2005

The Young Avengers are a group of teenagers with special powers. There are:

- Iron Lad (Nathaniel Richards) – He founded the team and is a scientific genius. He wears an armoured suit that he can control with his mind. He leaves the team to become Kang.
- Wiccan (Billy Kaplan) – He has magical abilities and is an original member of the Young Avengers.

- Stature (Cassie Lang) – She can change size and is also a member of the Mighty Avengers.
- Hulkling (Teddy Altman) – He is a shapeshifter and was one of the original members. He has the ability to heal.
- Patriot (Eli Bradley) – He is the grandson of Isaiah Bradley and at first doesn't have any superhero abilities but later gets them from a blood transfusion with his grandad. He is also one of the original members.
- Hawkeye (Kate Bishop) – She is a skilled archer and swordswoman. She joined the team after helping them out during a rescue mission.
- Speed (Tommy Shepherd) – He is extremely fast and can accelerate and destabilise atoms. It is thought that he might be the twin brother of Wiccan.
- The team also had a member called Vision for a time. It would be great if they had their own movie one day.

Z IS FOR...

- To date there have been no appearances of Zauriel in any TV show or film
- Powers: Ability to fly, speak to animals
- First comic-book appearance: June 1997

Zauriel was a guardian angel in Heaven until he was forced to leave by supporters of the rebel Asmodel. He landed on Earth and has stayed there ever since. He still has his wings but he no longer has immortality. He became a member of the Justice League and is good friends with Aquaman but later decided to go it alone. Zauriel might no longer have his angelic sonic cry but he can still communicate with animals.